Stephan Schiffman's
Telemarketing

Stephan Schiffman's
Telemarketing

BOB ADAMS, INC.
PUBLISHERS
Holbrook, Massachusetts

Published by Adams Media Corporation
260 Center Street, Holbrook, MA 02343

ISBN: 1-55850-130-4

Printed in Canada

J   I   H   G   F   E

This publication is designed to provide accurate and authoritative information with
regard to the subject matter covered. It is sold with the understanding that the publisher
is not engaged in rendering legal, accounting, or other professional advice. If legal
advice or other expert assistance is required, the services of a competent professional
person should be sought.
— From a *Declaration of Principles* jointly adopted by a Committee of the
American Bar Association and a Committee of Publishers and Associations

COVER PHOTO: The Ira Rosen Studio, South Bellmore, NY

This book is available at quantity discounts for bulk purchases.
For information, call 1-800-872-5627 (in Massachusetts, 781-767-8100).

Visit our home page at http://www.adamsmedia.com

DEDICATION

To AFS, again.

ACKNOWLEDGMENTS

Grateful thanks are due to the many people in the Bob Adams organization who, over the years, have provided invaluable insights on the materials and concepts presented in this and other books. These include Chris Ciaschini, Brandon Toropov, Peter Gouck, and Gigi Ranno.

TABLE OF CONTENTS

CHAPTER FIFTEEN

APPENDIX

The world belongs
to the enthusiast
who keeps cool.

— *William McFee*

INTRODUCTION

About five years ago I decided to learn to play golf.

It's a great game. It's not for everyone, of course, but I had been a fan for long enough that I knew I really wanted to get the hang of playing it myself. So I signed up for some lessons with a pro at a local country club.

There's a great deal that goes into a good golf swing. Bending in. Addressing the ball. Following through. If you've been playing the game for years, these things become second nature. But I hadn't been playing for years. I was starting from scratch, and the things the pro was asking me to do felt awkward to say the least.

"Stick with it," he told me toward the end of my first lesson. "You'll get the feel. Practice next Sunday using what I've taught you here, then let's try another lesson two weeks from now."

It seemed like sensible enough advice. But that Sunday on the green, I ignored it. It was my course time, after all—who was to say I couldn't swing the way I felt like swinging? Certainly I could remember those silly instructions whenever it suited me—couldn't I?

Can you guess what kind of golf scores I posted that Sunday?

You're going to have to, because I certainly don't intend to publicize them here. Lousy golf scores or no lousy golf scores, though, I found that I had another problem. When I got back to my lesson with the pro the following weekend, it was immediately clear that I was not ready for the second lesson yet. I was still waiting for the first one. The fundamentals we had discussed previously were still beyond my grasp.

Just to recap my little adventure, then, I took my first lesson with the pro, got some good information on the basics, decided not to apply those basic principles on the golf course, and then discovered that the net result of my decision to reinvent the game of golf was that I might as well have skipped the initial lesson.

The moral is, learn the basics before you try to reinvent the game. That's good advice for golf, and it's good advice for phone sales work, too.

There's a lot of information in this book. I'm going to work on the assumption that you bought it so you could get the most you possibly could from that information—and increase your earnings potential as a telemarketer (or help others to do so). I hope you'll profit from my golfing mistake and follow through on the basics you'll find between these covers. I hope you *won't* do as I did and try to reinvent *your* game after you file the information in that infamous "it-sounds-good-in-theory" file we all have in our heads.

Theory is meaningless. Practice is what builds skills. If the skill you hope to develop is that of earning significantly more money over the phone than you now do, I firmly believe you've got the right book for it. But just reading the words won't do the trick for you. You have to work the ideas into your real-life sales patterns.

At first, it may not feel right. You may think to yourself, "This is uncomfortable—it's not the way I'm used to doing things." That's okay. I had exactly the same feeling after my first golf lesson. If you keep plugging away at the basics, they really will become second nature to you in a very short time. And your performance will, I assure you, improve dramatically in the long term.

Any new undertaking requires some initial open-mindedness. The techniques described in this book are no exception.

As elsewhere in life, learning what works is only half the battle. Unlearning what *doesn't* work is the other half. And when it comes to telemarketing, there's plenty that doesn't work.

◆　　◆　　◆

Much of what is being taught to today's telemarketers—if, indeed, they are taught anything at all—is garbage.

Please pardon my frankness on this point. But I think you'll probably agree, given your own experience with telephone sales people, that my assessment is an accurate one.

Most contemporary telemarketing training encourages salespeople to:

- ◆ Sound like automatons

- ◆ Treat all prospects as though they were identical

- ◆ Ask prospects questions for which no groundwork has been laid

- ◆ Interrupt prospects

- ◆ Read directly from a script with no spontaneity

- ◆ Use heavy-handed, high-pressure techniques

- ◆ Focus on short-term results rather than long-term relationships

- ◆ Focus on making a high volume of calls at the expense of making quality calls

- ◆ Insult the prospect's intelligence

- ◆ Turn potentially productive conversations into arguments

- ◆ Establish little or no credibility

- ◆ Assume that what works for other telemarketers will work for them

- ◆ Focus on the objective of the call rather than prospect needs

- ◆ Sell products or services about which they know next to nothing and have typically never used

- ◆ Encourage both the telemarketer and the company to waste resources (time and money respectively) by "sending information" to unqualified, uninterested prospects

I could go on, but you get the idea. The proposition that most of today's phone sales campaigns are intrusive, annoying, amateurish, and self-centered isn't one that's likely to be challenged by anyone who answers the phone on a regular basis.

The many, many problems people on the receiving end of telemarketing calls have with phone sales have, in my view, nothing to do with telephone communication as a commercial medium. On the contrary, these problems have everything to do with the *inadequate, improperly focused, or nonexistent training* telemarketers receive.

To my way of thinking, a salesperson is a little like a physician. Just as a doctor does, the salesperson must analyze a person's present condition, draw conclusions, and help implement solutions to any problems that are discovered. If there were an army of self-proclaimed "doctors" out there with inadequate training, making ill-considered diagnoses, and, frequently, offering ludicrously wrong treatment recommendations, you and I simply wouldn't stand for it.

Today's ill-managed telemarketing campaigns are whipping up similarly strong feelings of resentment, and it's no surprise. People know proficiency when they hear it, and most of the time they're *not* hearing it from the telemarketers who call them.

◆   ◆   ◆

This book is not a panacea. It's a tool.

It's addressed to the thousands upon thousands of salespeople who make their living by telephoning sales prospects. It offers solid advice on improving performance for those who must attempt to close sales over the phone, and it also has some important ideas for those who schedule appointments or do other non-closing sales work by telephone.

I'm not saying this book has all the answers for all the potential selling situations all telemarketers may encounter. Providing those answers is not my purpose. An A-to-Z approach to the hundreds of different markets, regions, and products telemarketers face would be long, unwieldy, and 99% useless to any given reader. What I do propose, however, is that the basic principles embodied in this book will help anyone who sells by phone to promote a partnership-based, high-credibility professional image over the phone. And someone who makes calls using this approach is going to have, almost automatically, a powerful competitive edge these days. Can you guess why?

Because almost everyone else
is missing the mark!

One of my favorite writers, a gentleman by the name of Arnold Bennett, once made a telling observation about this very subject. Bennett wrote, "When a thing is thoroughly well done, it often has the air of being a miracle." Nowadays, a polite, professional, well-informed telemarketer who thinks in the long term really does seem to the prospect like a miracle. And making that principle work for you is what this book is all about.

◆   ◆   ◆

In the pages that follow, we'll be discussing a lot of new ideas. Some of them may seem strange to you. All I ask is that you keep an open mind in reviewing them and give them an honest try.

This is especially important if you are reading this book as a means of imparting new ideas to an existing sales force. I'm not going to pretend for an instant that this book will be able to change the patterns of the vast majority of telemarketers overnight—but I do have hopes that the sales managers and other supervisors who read it will be able to pass along the main message here: Cooperation works, confrontation doesn't.

To those reading this book who are managers, involved in the decisions that affect the lives of salespeople, I ask that you stop for a moment and take a good look around your company. Ask yourself some hard questions.

- ◆ Are your salespeople in for the long haul—or are they likely to leave a matter of months (or weeks) due to burnout?

- ◆ Do they take a positive, upbeat, problem-solving approach to building partnerships with prospects?

- ◆ Are their compensation packages competitive?

◆ Do they receive the courtesy and consideration due to professionals?

◆ Is their calling environment appealing and pleasant? (Could you yourself comfortably and happily work there?)

◆ Do they receive all the information necessary to satisfactorily resolve customer inquiries on a timely basis?

All too often, the answers to these questions are "no." If you are in a position to change that state of affairs, I want to take this opportunity to ask you to strongly consider doing so.

Why am I making a request like that? It's selfish, really. I am a firm believer in the idea that no salesperson benefits from a tarnished public image of sales as a profession. Telemarketing, as you may know, suffers from a severe image problem—and I have to be frank with you, that bothers me. The stereotypical image of the telemarketer—combative, inexperienced, insincere—is what I have to train people to overcome. The less that image prevails, the easier my work as a trainer (and yours as a sales manager) becomes.

If that doesn't fly for you, I can offer an even better reason to improve the environment in your company. *Your salespeople will make more money* . . . and your company will, too.

— S.S.

PART I

SURVEYING THE LANDSCAPE

CHAPTER ONE

SWIMMING UPSTREAM

"Sales calls stink."

These days, that's the opinion of more and more of the people you as a telemarketer will be trying to turn into customers. It's not pretty, but it's true: There's an uphill battle ahead of you.

If you've done any telemarketing work at all—or even followed the news recently—you probably know that state legislatures are under increasing pressure nowadays to put more and more restrictions on selling by phone. Some politicians want to ban telemarketing outright. Why do you suppose that is?

Stop and think for a moment. How do *you* view sales-oriented telephone communications? Have you ever complained that your phone was ringing off the hook, or that you couldn't get a moment's peace because of all the calls you had to handle? Given that feeling, how do you react to the typical, amateurish sales call? Have you ever hung up in disgust at receiving one of those appeals?

If you're honest, you'll have to admit that your first re-action to the standard sales phone call is not positive. But that's not a reason to *abandon* phone sales. Far from it! You already have some idea of what you're up against—and what you cannot, under any circumstances, sound like. ("Congratulations! You have been selected as the lucky win-

ner of a fantastic new widget opportunity [click] . . . opportunity [click] . . . opportunity . . .")

◆   ◆   ◆

Selling by phone is not the same as it once was. For one
thing, people selling by phone in the early days had an important advantage you don't: novelty. In the postwar years,
when telemarketing as an industry first began to develop in
earnest, people tended to think of getting a telephone call as
something special, something that validated one's status
and feelings of high self-esteem. After all, for decades, people had thought of the telephone as something of a luxury
item. Today, of course, that's no longer the case. We've become so conditioned to using the telephone in virtually all
aspects of life that we take it for granted. Moreover, the pace
of life is so much more hectic than it once was that some of
us may even consider *any* telephone call an intrusion, at
least at first.

And let's face it: There are more telemarketers out there
now than in the past. The phone company recently issued a
report that estimated the number of sales calls placed to pri-
vate homes at eighteen million *per day*. Just as advertising
executives must devise new ways to rise above the "traffic"
of competing sales messages on television and through
other media, today's successful telemarketer must find
some means of standing out from the crowd and overcoming resentment associated with calls someone *else* made.
Whether you like it or not, the odds are that your prospect
has recently been approached by a telemarketer who had no
idea what he or she was doing. That makes your job harder.

Of course, telemarketers are not the only ones you're
competing against for attention. The average person receives *two thousand* selling messages during the course of

the day, via television, radio, magazines, newspapers, and other media. That's a lot of noise. Whatever you come up with to say to your prospect, it had better be arresting if it's going to compete with all those appeals to buy.

Nobody's crazy about receiving that many advertising messages, but most of us accept it as part of life in the late 20th century. Similarly, phone solicitations may never be exactly *popular*—in the sense of being something a person looks forward to—but they are a component of the modern economy. My guess is that telemarketers, even though they're easy targets for media figures and politicians, will never be legislated out of existence. It is important, though, for us to note the many new features of the landscape in which the telemarketing industry operates today.

We must accept that the telephone is no longer simply a way we communicate. It is a way we live our lives. Accordingly, those who use it are expected to meet a certain standard. They are expected to be brief and to the point; they are expected to use common courtesy at all times; and they are expected to make the most of the time on the line by talking *to* their partners rather than at (or, worse, through) them.

The Telephone: Your Tool for Success

Although it must be used responsibly to yield anything like meaningful long-term results, telephone communication remains a remarkably powerful medium. There are several reasons for this.

The first and most important reason behind the power of telephone communication is its *intrusiveness*. It never ceases to amaze me how, when I am giving a seminar to a room full of people, everything stops whenever a phone rings. It is as if, when a telephone rings, it is impossible for modern humans *not* to stop what they're doing until the receiver is picked up. That's a powerful call to attention, one that focuses the spotlight on your message. By the same token, if what you are interrupting is perceived as more important than what you have to say, you'll have difficulty commanding the prospect's attention.

There is, in addition, a sense of *urgency* to most contemporary business telephone communications, and this, too, can be made to work in your favor. The next time your phone rings, take a moment to note your own reactions. Isn't there a sense of excitement, a feeling that the call may bear important news—news you want to learn about as soon as possible? It could be a customer! It could be your boss! It could be anybody! Think about it. If you're in a meeting with someone and your phone rings, don't you take the call—even if another person is there? Take this "it-could-be-important" factor and add to it the intense time pressure felt by many professionals, and you have a high-expectation, low-patience attitude—a desire to get to the crucial news quickly. Used properly, this expectant attitude of prospects can aid your cause immensely. Used improperly, it will earn you the sound of a receiver being slammed onto the hook.

Finally, telephone communications are *controllable*, at least from the standpoint of image projection. Let me explain what I mean by that. If you make an in-person presentation to a prospect, there are a great many variables you will have to attend to. You will have to select a good set of clothes, be sure your hair is groomed properly, eliminate any potentially distracting nervous tics, be sure your hands are dry when the two of you shake hands, and so on. All of these interpersonal cues, and dozens of others, will be important for you to manage if you want to send an image of confidence, competence, and poise during the meeting. However, if you are making a presentation by phone, there is only *one* major variable for you to attend to: your voice. Assuming equal levels of product knowledge, a qualified phone sales rep has far fewer image-related concerns than an equally qualified rep who must prepare for a face-to-face meeting. Now, there are certainly some things about selling by phone that are more challenging than in-person work, but it's nice to know that at least one factor is working in your favor!

You Are a Professional

Anybody can make a sale. Only a professional can have a sales career.

I firmly believe that the reason so many of today's telemarketers sound so completely unprofessional is that they think of themselves as being unprofessional. They don't want to be doing what they're doing, and you can hear it from word one. They have failed to cultivate a solid business-oriented self-image. Once you've completed this book—if you follow all the instructions I pass along—you will not have that problem.

The salesperson's ability to control his or her image over the phone is something of a double-edged sword. If you take the steps necessary to project a positive image over the telephone, it is comparatively easy to do so. On the other hand, if you have a negative attitude about your position, that will almost always be apparent to your prospect.

I am a firm believer in the principle that you can't cheat in the long term (and probably not in the short term, either) when it comes to dealing with people on the phone. Sooner or later—probably sooner—people pick up on insincerity. If you don't feel comfortable trying to sell them something, they aren't going to feel comfortable buying it from you.

During the decade of the eighties, there were a lot of high-gloss, low-principle telemarketers selling everything from penny stocks to discount travel packages. They bulldozed past everything in their way. They kept their eye on their own bottom line. They thought company loyalty, customer needs, and integrity were things of the past. Now they find it is their sales careers that are things of the past. Don't follow their example. Be a survivor. Be a customer-first team player whose word can be counted on.

Today's successful telemarketers tend to be *confident, relaxed professionals whose main goal is to find as many ways as possible to help people solve their problems via a worthwhile product or service.* They just happen to do their job by phone.

Successful telemarketers *don't* mark time until a "real job" comes along. (If your job isn't "real," your prospect will almost certainly sense that in short order.) They don't over-compensate for a lack of selling skills with a hyper-polished, overbearing delivery. (Doing so is part of what gives the telemarketing industry such a bad image.) And they don't lie—period. (If you are selling a product or service that you *know* is unlikely to do what you say it will, get another job. There is nothing in this book that will help you overcome that hurdle.)

There is, to be sure, some unethical activity in the telemarketing field today. Better Business Bureaus around the country are doing a pretty good job of keeping track of the bad apples, however. You might want to contact your local Bureau if you have any questions about a current or prospective employer. I strongly suggest that you stay away from quick-buck outfits. They exploit not only their customers, but you the telemarketer as well. All those people who sold penny stocks from boiler rooms are out of work now!

There's one more great reason for you to view telemarketing as a professional partnership: survival. I work with a lot of sales forces, and I'm here to tell you that the salespeople who succeed over time—the ones who survive shifting business climates and recessions and company restructurings—are those who cultivate a professional self-image and see the object of their work as to help others. I can't reproduce any scientific study for you that proves that, but I can tell you it's the unmistakable pattern I've seen after working with literally hundreds of thousands of salespeople over the years.

CHAPTER TWO

THE GAME

Let's pretend for a moment that you've become a tennis fanatic.

You've read up on tennis, checking out every volume in your local library that contains even a passing reference to the sport. You've bought tennis videos and watched them over and over again. You've practiced the moves of the world's best tennis players in your living room and, alone, at a local court after work. You know tennis inside and out, and you're ready to play.

No matter how much preparation you do, though, you still need a partner to play with. And if you're going to get anything meaningful out of the game, you're going to have to know the types of moves your partner is likely to show you.

In telemarketing, too, you need to have someone—someone on the other end of the phone. Your effort is pointless without that other person. In a way, I admit, my comparison of sales with tennis—or any sporting contest—comes up short, because the objective is not to *defeat* the customer, but to find a way to work with him or her. Nevertheless, I'll stick by this analogy for one important reason: *during the tennis game, it's a fairly safe bet that your partner is going to send the ball careening toward you.* That had better not come as a surprise. Your ability to react to the various angles and speeds and rotations will, ultimately, be a function of the amount of time you've spent "on the court." But good pregame practice and preparation can go a long way toward helping you build up a solid game.

I'd like you to take a moment now to think of the things in telemarketing that you can be pretty sure are going to happen, no matter what.

For one thing, you can be confident that the people you talk to are not going to be waiting by the phone with bated breath, hoping you'll call. Some of the people you talk to are going to express an initial annoyance. Some may be hostile. Some may hang up on you.

Other people will offer you objections. (As we will see, this is often a positive rather than a negative sign.) They will outline reasons the product or service doesn't seem right for them. It's a good bet that the majority of these objections will be familiar to you from your past telemarketing experience. (If you are new to the field, you will probably notice the broad categories into which objections fall after only a few days or weeks of calling.)

Still others will react positively to your message. They will want to hear more about your product or service—and, again, they will generally do so along predictable lines if you've been selling for any meaningful length of time.

The point is that the vast majority of reactions we encounter will be ones we can anticipate. That will be the main of the system you will find outlined in this book. Our first and most powerful weapon will be the *use of past experience to enhance our ability to react to present situations.*

Getting Off Book

This implies a certain flexibilty, of course—which brings me to the topic of the script.

As we will soon learn, a basic script is essential. But I define a "basic script" as one from which you can deviate as occasion demands. *Nothing* that follows here is likely to work for you if your telemarketing consists of reading a script word-for-word. If this is the way you work now, I'm going to ask you to change it. (You can show this part of the book to your supervisor if you feel that will help.) Reading a "canned" presentation verbatim is generally the single most annoying thing you can do to a prospect. There are a few gifted salespeople who can pull it off and make it sound natural—but that only proves the point! You *want* to sound natural, not like an automaton. If the first thing your prospect hears is a monotonous recitation of words and phrases that sound unreal to both of you, then the words really *are* foreign. I mean that quite sincerely. By draining all the life from your presentation, you are speaking a language the prospect has no interest in. You are, when you come right down to it, asking the prospect to terminate the conversation as quickly as possible. These days, prospects have no problem honoring your request.

Again—how do you react when you pick up a ringing phone and hear only mindless, rote blathering instead of conversation? Doesn't it make you feel there's not the slightest chance that anything you say will have any effect on the message you'll receive, because the person will probably pick up exactly where he or she left off—regardless of what you have to say? And how do you feel when you receive a recorded sales message, but initially mistake it for a bad, living telemarketer? Doesn't that common mistake tell you something about the way word-for-word sales appeals are perceived?

A conversational approach to interaction with the prospect is absolutely essential to a competitive approach to telemarketing. That may not always have been the case, but it certainly is today. There is enough of the impersonal, the scattershot, the insincere in our everyday life. We must offer the prospect an ally—not a computer printout.

If none of that has convinced you yet to lay off the canned presentation, try this: *too many short-sighted people are still doing it now and rapidly extinguishing what little patience may remain with this tired, outdated approach.* Those people are your competition. Let them make the mistakes. Don't follow them down this road.

I know of one charitable organization that had some real problems with its telemarketing campaign. They kept missing their targets, but they couldn't figure out why. The second I listened to their reps on the phone, though, I sure could tell what the problem was. The people were charging through their scripts at breakneck speed—and they sounded not just hurried, but dishonest! Here they were trying to raise funds for a veteran's organization that was as legitimate as legitimate causes get, a group that had been around for decades. Yet the telemarketers all sounded like high-pressure, quick-buck automatons.

I sat down with the sales manager and told him where his people were going wrong. "Your prospects," I said, "think you guys are flim-flam artists. They don't believe this is a legitimate charity—because you don't *sound* like a legitimate charity! Your people sound insincere. What's worse, they sound like they're bombing through their script at a mile a minute because they expect the police to break down the door any second!"

The problem was no sooner identified than resolved. I think this anecdote will give you an idea of the importance of sending a message that resonates truly with your prospect.

Developing an Image

Advertising agencies launch multi-million-dollar campaigns to help you become familiar with some market entities, usually at the expense of other entities. If you're like most of us, you've been bombarded with countless messages designed to make it easier for you to develop a specific type of awareness about the airline that flies the friendly skies, the rental car service that tries harder, the investment firm that makes its money the old-fashioned way, and hundreds, perhaps thousands of others. What the advertising firms are facing is a glut of claimants for your attention—and their quandary is not at all unlike the one you face as a telemarketer.

Advertisers must use their media—television, newspapers, magazine, radios, billboards, and so on—to develop what is known as "top of the mind awareness," that familiarity with a basic concept that enables recipients to associate a message with its recognized sender. You must use your medium—the telephone—to craft a unique, legitimate image that will serve the same purpose. The scale may be smaller, but the principle is exactly the same.

Put more plainly, you must find a way to keep the prospect from considering your contact with him to be just another annoying sales call. You will do that by creating a distinctive telephone image. *Every* telemarketer, in today's market, must face up to the problem of setting himself or herself apart from the pack. Failing to do so will yield substandard sales results and, more than likely, early burnout.

The first steps we will take in developing that image concern not the sounds or phrases of the call, but you.

Critical Review: Dress

What do you typically wear to work?

I ask that question of some of the more rumpled telemarketers who come my way and receive a bemused shrug that seems to say, "Whatever's handy." I tend to find, though, that not only are these telemarketers rumpled; their days tend to progress in a rumpled, unkempt kind of way, too. And—stop the presses—their monthly sales totals often look a little worse for wear and tear, just like their wardrobes. Remember, we are talking about professional salespeople who *just happen to sell over the phone.*

Earlier on, when I pointed out the advantage of the controllable image in telemarketing, you may have found yourself thinking something along these lines: "Great! I can make the calls in my underwear! All that matters is my voice!"

Well, your sales manager may have something to say about that approach. Actually, I do, too. While it's true you don't have to worry as much about the direct nonvocal messages you send to the *prospect* on the phone, you do have to be careful about the messages you send yourself!

In this part of the book, I am asking you to take a couple of simple, specific steps that will help you maintain an upbeat, can-do approach to the day. Chief among them is the use of clothing to send a powerful message of competence and control to the most important person you'll work with all day: you.

Put aside the sweaters with holes worn in the elbows, the shirts with inkstains, the socks that don't match, and all the rest of the second-hand, second-rate apparel. Invest in a sharp addition or two to your wardrobe. Get a few reasonably priced garments and/or accessories that tell the world at large—and the person who occupies your desk—that you mean business.

While you're at it, take another look at your hair, nails, and other aspects of personal grooming. When you look in the mirror, do you see a clean, neat, approachable professional smiling back at you? If not, make the appropriate changes.

Critical Review: Your Calling Area

What does your work area look like? Is it a maze of coffee cups, unframed photos, indecipherable notes, and year-old magazines? If so, you're not sending the right signals to yourself.

Your work area should fairly shout that you are a well-organized, self-motivated person who knows the difference between coping and excelling. If your area is disorganized or shows signs of neglect, the message you are sending to others and yourself is that you don't care enough about your surroundings to attend to them. In short, you are saying that you show up because you *have to*, not because you want to, and that you will do the absolute minimum in terms of upkeep. Those aren't positive signals, and issuing positive signals, as you've probably already deduced, is the first and most important step in forming your professional phone image.

Some will argue that a messy work area is a sign of a creative mind. That may well be. But if I'm given the choice between fostering creativity in this way or increasing sales, I'm going to pick upping my sales totals every time. Experience has shown that the vast majority of salespeople can only benefit from keeping a well organized work area.

I also suggest that you purchase a small mirror and hang it where you can see it when you make calls. There's a very good reason for this. If you can see yourself in the mirror, you can tell whether or not you're smiling and upbeat. If you're not smiling, you won't sound to the prospect as if you're smiling and upbeat! (You really can tell over the phone when a caller is glum and downbeat; the mirror method is a guaranteed solution to that problem.) One telemarketing sales organization purchased 2500 mirrors for their salespeople at my suggestion. Their sales are up.

Critical Review: Your Emotional Cycles

As you progress through the day's calls, try to monitor your own emotional state. Is each call easy in the morning, but a chore later in the day? Is there a point when the calls all seem to take on the same numbing sound to you? Perhaps you have a daily rhythm whereby the earlier calls are ones you look forward to— but you dread that rut you always run into in the afternoon.

These types of cycles are almost always self-perpetu-
ated. I knew one telemarketing salesperson who was great
for one sale a night, but would then freeze up at the thought
of closing that second sale. Sure enough, the second sale
was an elusive item indeed. This lasted for weeks. It was obviously a mental problem, and that very fact made the hurdle more difficult to overcome. My feeling was that the cycle
had been allowed to present itself early and never challenged. After two or three nights of closing only the first
sale, this salesperson's subconscious mind had found a
great reason not to sell: the Second Sale Jinx! The self-per-
petuating fear of being unable to close that second sale grew
like a seedling, until it was eventually a nice strong weed. I
got him out of the cycle by making him take a coffee break
after his first sale one night, then telling him to pretend he
was starting the night over fresh.

The point is, you have to know what your unproduc-
tive cycles are before you can do anything about them. For
now, just ask yourself: Is there any point in the day at which
my sales work seems stale, uninspiring, or even unduly
frightening? When do these cycles take place?

If changing your negative pattern proves difficult, you
can rearrange your schedule. Spend your day in such a way
as to increase your positive time and minimize or eliminate
the amount of time you spend reconfirming negatives (like
"My last calls of the morning never seem to go well").

Critical Review: Thought Management

What is thought management? It's positive self-affirma-
tion. It's sending unambiguous positive messages to yourself, particularly when things don't seem to be going well.
It's taking the responsibility for compensating for negative
comments you may hear over the phone by making a point
of telling yourself things like:

My product helps people.

♦ I have a solid, confident style.

♦ This is a great day.

♦ This is the right company for me.

♦ I can do anything I set my mind to.

Issuing such affirmations is one of the chief distinguishing characteristics of successful people. You may even want to have one of the messages you find most meaningful printed and framed.

Critical Review: Your Calling Routine

Are you one of those salespeople who sits down at nine in the morning, picks up the phone, and "warms up" with real, live prospects? If so, you're throwing away money. Try to establish a regular practice routine—say, by role-playing with a fellow salesperson—that will help you get the fog to lift and the bugs to depart *before* you talk to someone whose perception of you will affect your paycheck.

This is a vitally important step that far too many of today's telemarketers ignore.

Critical Review: Your Product or Service

Do you really know what it is you're selling? That is to say, are you familiar describing it to a customer, in user's terms, in intimate detail? Some make the mistake of describing products or services from the point of view of the person designing or testing them; that's not what this is about. Can you use simple, everyday language to make a compelling first-hand assessment of the item or program in question? Try to learn as much as you possibly can about the product or service you are offering. If at all possible, try to use it in exactly the same way a customer would. When you speak from first-hand experience about the items you are trying to sell, it is much easier to make statements you know you can stand behind.

In addition to taking a good, close look at your product or service, review all the sales materials presented to prospective customers. (It never ceases to amaze me how many salespeople never bother to read the circulars they send out to customers!) Does your sales literature prominently feature your name and contact information, as well as information about the best time to reach you? It should.

Come to some conclusions about the people who actually use your product or service. Are they primarily older? Younger? High-income? Middle-income? Men? Women? Sports fans? Voracious readers? For professional telemarketers, the days of ramrodding sales through, of signing up people about whom you know nothing, have passed.

Perhaps you're an entrepreneur or are similarly engaged in the sale of an exciting idea rather than a tangible product. Are you genuinely excited about this idea? Is your excitement contagious? Can other people tell instantly what it is about your approach that makes it worth looking at? Can you sum up in a single sentence the most exciting component of the idea to which you've committed yourself?

Critical Review: Your Company

In the pages that follow, you'll be asked to give the prospect a brief summation of what your company does best. This means that you must *know* what it is your company does best; if you have any doubts whatsoever, you should dispel them now by asking to review the appropriate literature: annual reports, mission statements, or advertising circulars are good places to start. If these are unavailable or don't tell you enough, ask your superior to give you a verbal overview of the company and its history.

Try to find some legitimate superlative you can apply to the firm you work for. Is your company the largest competitor in its market(s)? The most prolific? The most innovative? The most efficient? The most economical? The easiest to work with? The producer of the highest-quality products?

The Total Package

Competence. Authority. Control.

These three elusive factors are what you want to project when you make your calls, but you can only do so if you have taken the time to do a comprehensive personal inventory. Taken together, the critical reviews I have outlined above form the first crucial steps in developing a positive professional self-image that radiates competence, authority, and control. In addition, these steps will help you harness your own personal motivitational abilities. Over time, you will see that the best answer to the question "How do I keep myself motivated?" is one you yourself come up with after following the review guidelines I've just given you.

Don't skip these steps and proceed to the rest of the book! It is only through commitment to the ongoing process of personal development that you will get the results you desire. There is no magic wand to wave over your telephone that will improve your sales. Your objective is to improve the way you handle the only instruments over which you have complete control: yourself and your attitude. Follow the instruction in this chapter and you will be well on the way to mastering those tools.

Believe me, it's a proven formula. Dress like a professional, act like a professional, *think* like a professional—and you will be a professional.

CHAPTER THREE

LISTENING TO YOU

This brief chapter is about another critical review, one that you should carry out *after* you have attended to the ones listed in the previous chapter. It has to do with your voice.

If you don't already have one, buy or borrow a tape recorder and record your standard presentation. (If you haven't yet developed one, read a passage from this book.)

I've found that 90-95% of all telemarketers have never recorded their sales pitch and listened to it critically. Perhaps you are reticent about doing this. I'm going to ask you to do it anyway, and here are my reasons why.

◆ There is no earthly reason for you *not* to know what you sound like to the prospect.

◆ You may have conversational tics (such as stammering or repeating yourself) or use annoying filler words (such as "um," "er," and "y'know"). If you are aware of these problems, you can correct them. If you aren't aware of them, you can't—and you will *definitely* lose sales.

◆ You may be unaware of problems with rhythm or pace. A delivery that is too slow will destroy interest; one that is too fast will annoy your prospect and make your message hard to understand. Again, failing to correct problems like these costs you money.

◆ If you have never listened to your voice on tape, you almost certainly have problems with tonal variation. A good telemarketing pitch must incorporate subtle distinctions in vocal delivery. A flat monotone is simply unappealing.

◆ You may tend to steamroll people. You will probably be able to determine this by listening to your side of the conversation on tape. The call you are making is nothing more or less than *a conversation with a peer about a subject of mutual interest!* If it sounds like a sermon or a battlefield lecture, you will need to make some adjustments.

I could go on, but I think you get the message. You are putting yourself at a distinct disadvantage if you decline to listen to your own vocal delivery on tape. If you find the experience humbling, remember that most people are not fond of the sound of their own recorded voice. Keep your attention focused on whether you display the kinds of technical flaws outlined above, rather than on solving any aesthetic problems you may have with your voice.

Don't try to alter your natural voice or accent unless you are a trained actor or an expert in phonetics. You run a much greater risk of sounding contrived and artificial than of stumbling upon a "new you" guaranteed to generate sales. The objective here is not to discard your existing vocal habits, but to improve them by spotting manifest problems in delivery.

In short, you must be yourself on the phone—but remove any of the obstacles that may keep your prospect from hearing that genuine you.

CHAPTER FOUR

THE TYPES OF CALLS

In this chapter, we're going to examine the six major types of telemarketing calls and determine, for each one, what the telemarketer's focus is. In the next chapter, we'll look in more detail at the overall sales cycle into which these calls fit.

1: The Freestanding Closing Call

When you make this kind of call, your aim is get a commitment from the prospect to purchase the product or service right then and there, over the phone. More and more things are being sold in this way, including some categories of merchandise that only a few years ago would have seemed to demand face-to-face encounters.

This type of call is covered in detail in the following chapters on the sales cycle and script development.

2: The Appointment Call

When you make this kind of call, your aim is to set an appointment for yourself or another sales representative. At the face-to-face meeting, the prospect will hear a direct presentation regarding the product or service. Of course, you are not attempting to "close" during the call meant to set up the appointment. (In some business areas, sales managers will *insist* on sending the sales rep along for the face-to-face meeting, even if the prospect tells you over the phone that he or she is definitely sold and doesn't need to meet with anyone.)

This type of call is covered in detail in a later chapter of the book.

3: The Post-Visit Closing Call

This variation on the closing call is less common, but you do run across it from time to time. When you make this kind of call, your aim is to follow up on an in-person visit and close the sale over the phone.

The general guidelines for this call are the same as those for the freestanding closing call. Only minor (and obvious) variations will be necessary to adapt it to your needs.

4: The Lead Development Call

When you make this kind of call, your aim is to initiate a relationship, period. You do not anticipate trying to close a sale; instead, you focus on developing the prospect's knowledge and awareness of you, the product or service, and the company. Guidelines for this type of call will vary widely from industry to industry and market to market. Intense customization is usually necessary. You are best advised to talk to a sales manager or senior sales person in your field for specific advice on how best to make these calls and incorporate them into your daily pattern.

5: The Follow-Up Call After Mailing Requested Information

When you make this kind of call, your aim is to turn the prospect's interest into action. Typically, that action is either scheduling an appointment to talk about the product or service in person or committing to a purchase agreement. I should note here that I am generally very skeptical about "sending information." If you think about it, you'll probably have to admit that agreeing to let a telemarketer "send information" is more often than not just a painless way to get him or her off the phone when there is no real interest. (And if you think about it some more, you'll probably have to admit that you yourself have used this dodge a few times!) However, I recognize that, particularly when it comes to dealing with prospects you never see, it is sometimes imperative to send tangible supporting material. I do suggest that you carefully screen all your "requests" for true interest in the product or service in question. You can do this by asking the prospect to specify the types of applications he or she forecasts. If, instead of more detailed information about problems, you receive a hastily improvised non-problem or a curt attempt to bring the conversation to a close, you'll know you're looking at wasted postage. Only send mail when you are sure there is a legitimate need or interest.

Admittedly, being sure of such things is an inexact science at best. This is the main reason this type of call is fundamentally a numbers game. Many of the prospects you speak to will be quite genial, but will go along with the idea of sending information simply to get you off the phone; others will represent legitimate sales opportunities. A good rule of thumb in taking the next step with this type of lead by phone is that you should be able to close—and close easily—the majority of the people who accept your follow-up call. (Be forewarned, however: Statistics have shown that most people you mail to will avoid doing so. If nothing else, this phenomenon will clear up the mystery of which prospects were being less than forthright.)

The best way to approach the close by phone in this situation is to draw the prospect out. Assume that the materials made it into the prospect's hands and focus on his or her reactions to the new information. You will be able to sense in short order whether or not it is time to close. Asking "whether or not the package made it through" is a yes-or-no query that will probably undercut your progress. Better to ask, "Mr. Jones, I don't know if you had the chance to notice the passage on page three about the incredibly low retrofitting costs for our widgets. Is that something that would be of benefit to your company?" Then follow up with a real-world success story about your product or service.

6: The Cold Follow-up Call After Mailing Unrequested Information

When you make this kind of call, your aim is to determine if a blanket mailing has succeeded in building interest in the product or service *or* to develop interest among recipients who do not recall receiving the blanket mailing. In either case, you will typically seek to set an in-person appointment or attempt to close the sale over the phone.

The guidelines supplied for call type #5 can generally be adapted with success here. The closing rate is, predictably, somewhat lower. Nevertheless, a good phone follow-up campaign can often double a mass mailing's effectiveness. (Some firms I know of have posted astronomical conversion rates of 15-20% by using proper follow-up.)

Your call should be made approximately seven days after the mailing piece is sent (assuming that it is sent first class, presorted.)

7: The Follow-up Call in Response to a Query for More Information Arising from a Direct Mailing

When you make this type of call, your aim is typically to act on the expression of interest and convert it into an appointment or sale.

All the respondent will have done by the time you speak to him or her is express an interest in the product or service. It is a common error to assume that the prospect is "ready to buy" when you call. In fact, it is still necessary to learn about the prospect's needs and make a presentation before attempting to close the sale.

The guidelines supplied for call type #5 can generally be adapted with success here; however, it should be understood that the "screening" process is usually unnecessary. The vast majority of the leads you act on in calls of this kind are qualified leads. (As a side note, let me point out that your best approach in developing an opening statement for these prospects should be to reinforce the idea that they made the right choice in responding to your mailing: "Mr. Smith, I'm happy to say that I received the card you sent in to us—and I have to say that a lot of people have gotten in contact with us over the past few days. Many of them are taking advantage of what we have to offer them, too.")

A Word About Sending Materials to Phone Prospects by Mail

As we have seen, the mailing of sales literature is often important to the progress of your phone sales work. At the same time, it is impossible to deny that many sales reps get caught in the trap of wasting massive amounts of time, effort, and company money by sending literature to unqualified prospects.

I strongly suggest that you follow a simple principle in dealing with the issue of sending sales literature.

> Send literature only as a result of the information you receive from the prospect over the phone. Do not make "mailing out the literature" the objective of any call. Remember that the more specific the mail you send is to the prospect's needs, the better the results will be. *Get* information before you *send* information.

Which Call Do You Make Most?

Most telemarketers make a certain type of call much more frequently than any other. Please review the above list to find the one—or perhaps two—you are most likely to make during the course of the day. Once you have identified your typical calling pattern(s), you will be ready to review the overall sales cycle discussed in the next chapter.

CHAPTER FIVE

THE FOUR STAGES

Although there are a number of different types of sales calls, all *sales* can be broken down into four distinct stages.

Every sale is different, of course, as is every selling environment. But each of the stages I'll be outlining in this chapter will be relevant to your telemarketing work. Depending on the market, the product or service, and the customer, it is possible for each of the stages to take place during a single call; by the same token, it's possible that it will take you a number of calls and/or scheduled visits to progress from one stage to the next. For the purposes of this chapter, we'll assume that all of the stages will be handled in one call. (If only life were so predictable for all salespeople!)

Each stage is intimately related to the entire process. The four stages link together neatly, so that you always know what your overall goal is. If you are in the first stage, your goal is to progress to the second stage. If you are in the second, you want to move on to the third. If you have progressed to the third, your aim is to move on to the final stage.

Stage One: Qualifying

You and your potential customer work together to determine that each party is interested in working with the other and in moving along in the sales cycle. Of course, you're not at all sure at this stage that the person on the phone is interested in buying what you have to offer. This certainty will only come with Stage Four—Closing.

It is a common error to mistake interest in pursuing discussions about what you have to offer with the imminent commitment to purchase. In the first stage, you are simply verifying that the prospect is willing to discuss the possible advantages of signing on with you. At the same time, you are checking to see whether the person or firm in question is the kind of account you hope to win. (Believe me, there are a great many manipulative, unprofessional "prospects" out there who will only cost you time, money, and aggravation. I'm not suggesting that you get F.B.I. dossiers on everyone you come in contact with, but only that you make sure you have a good gut feeling about the prospect before you move through the cycle with him or her.)

What could the first stage sound like? Let's take a look at an example.

Mr. Smith: Mr. Smith here.

　　You: Hi, Mr. Smith. Joan Peters here from the XYZ Widget Corporation. I'd like to ask you something about your widget service if I may.

Mr. Smith: Let me stop you right there, Joan. I really don't have any interest in going into that with you.

This point, a familiar one for anyone who has sold for more than fifteen minutes on the telephone, is perhaps the most difficult transition in all of telemarketing. Time after time, I find that it is in failing to overcome an initial objection such as the one above that the person trying to sell by phone really short-circuits his or her sales efforts. What to do?

Well, I submit to you that when Mr. Smith says something like this to you, he is really *not* talking about the product or service you have to offer. (At least not yet.) My guess is that he is really more interested in getting off the phone to focus on whatever he was working on just before you called. Given this state of affairs, you probably have about five seconds tops to get Mr. Smith's attention and get him to focus on your product or service.

I'm going to suggest you do this by using an All-Purpose Turnaround. It's best suited for this situation, but you'll be hearing a lot about this technique in other contexts later in the book. How do you use the All-Purpose Turnaround? All you do is point out to the person on the other end of the line that you've heard that objection before— from people who ended up becoming customers of yours. (Stop and think. Haven't you?)

> *You:* You know, Mr. Smith, a lot of people tell me that at first, before they got the chance to discuss in detail some of the benefits we're offering. What I'd like to do if I could is just ask you a couple of quick questions. Is that okay?
>
> *Mr. Smith:* Well . . . all right.

Perhaps this all seems too sudden for your calling environment. There is an interesting variation on the standard call that may help you. It involves restructuring your opening; you ask permission to tell the prospect a little bit about your company before you ask any questions about his or her background. This may be worth incorporating into your routine if you feel that proceeding directly into the information gathering stage is a little too intimidating for your prospect base.

> *You:* Mr. Smith, this is Joan Powers of ABC Manufacturing here, and I'm calling from Orchard Center to talk to the homeowners in the metro

Kansas City area to see if our products might be of service to them. Would it help if I told you a little bit about our company first? (Pause for breath.)

This approach can be quite successful if used properly. It takes advantage of a lingering question in the prospect's mind ("Who is this?"), and it will usually, but not always, garner a "Yes" response. That "Yes" is important. It builds trust and continuity.

Moreover, this "question mark" approach reinforces that the purpose of the call is to *help* the prospect. Note that you are not asking whether or not it is *convenient* for you to tell the prospect something about your firm, or whether it is *okay* for you to do so. You are asking whether or not it will *help* the prospect to evaluate what you have to offer if you take a moment to go into what your company is all about. Be sure you phrase the question in just this way.

This approach may be advisable if the prospects you are contacting are, because of the nature of your product or service, likely to associate your call with those "probing" telemarketing calls everyone hates—or, worse, the fraudulent "surveys" that are meant to dupe prospects into thinking they have at long last been selected to participate in a major national poll or ratings survey. People who have been fooled by such scams tend to be skeptical about "quick questions," and rightly so.

If you do elect to follow this route, keep the summary of your company brief and to the point. Use one or two sentences only, and focus on longevity, past success, and satisfied customers wherever you can do so. Then proceed to the next stage of the cycle by gaining the prospect's assent to your asking your (brief, nonthreatening, nondeceiving) questions designed to gather information for the presentation.

On those occasions where the prospects says that he or she would prefer *not* to hear about your firm in this stage, you can try to rescue the call in the following manner.

> *You:* Mr. Smith, this is Joan Powers of ABC Manufacturing here, and I'm calling from Orchard Center, talking to the homeowners in the metro Kansas City area to see if our products might be of service to them. Would it help if I told you a little bit about our company first?

> *Mr. Smith:* Joan, I appreciate your taking the time to call me today, but I'd rather not get into this.

> *You:* You know, I have to tell you, Mr. Smith, a lot of my current customers have reacted in just the same way before I had the chance to talk to them about what we had to offer. Do you mind if I ask you a very quick question or two?

Of course, it's important to note here that the All-Purpose Turnaround won't always do the trick. You will certainly have a number of conversations that go like this:

> . . . What I'd like to do if I could is just ask you a couple of quick questions. Is that okay?

> *Mr. Smith:* I told you. I'm not interested in talking to you. I don't care how quick your questions are. I've got to go.

What do you do? That will depend on your own selling environment. For most salespeople, however, there will definitely come a point at which you are best advised to *say "Thank you for your time," hang up, and make another call.* The whole point of Stage One is to determine whether or not Mr. Smith is a qualified lead and, if he is, to move along to Stage

Two with him. Don't badger him for helping you do just that! You've put the focus clearly on the product or service, and now, in an unmistakable way, Mr. Smith has answered your question. He is not interested in moving on to the next stage. Try again with someone else.

Try not to take it personally, either. Breathe deep. Send yourself a positive affirmation. Keep going.

Stage Two: Information Gathering

This is perhaps the most important stage, the one where you find out the needs of the individual in order to determine what courses of action will be taken later in the process. It's been estimated that 75% of the actual work of selling takes place at this point—the point at which the most important thing you can do is ask the proper questions and listen.

Managing this stage properly is one of the chief ways you can distinguish yourself from amateurish telemarketers, who typically have no interest in the prospect's perspective. They don't bother to determine how much or how little detail is appropriate to offer each prospect. They don't bother to ask what hurdles may exist with regard to the prospect's past experience. They don't bother to determine the prospect's level of knowledge about the problem they're supposedly trying to solve. They have a script. They have a phone. They can hear someone on the other end. They read.

Not you. You know that Stage Two is where you earn the *right* to make a later presentation. It is the point at which you say to the prospect, in so many words, "I care. This is the way I help people solve problems. The fact that I conduct my business over the telephone is incidental. What I'm really looking for is the best way to help you."

Around my office, we define "sales" as follows:

SALES: Asking people what they do, what they want, what they desire, and what they need—and then fulfilling those wants, desires, and needs with your product or service.

Obviously, Stage Two is the critical point at which this kind of selling really begins in earnest.

This stage is comparable to an in-person interview; as we've seen in the previous chapter, some people end the telemarketing phase of their job with Stage One once they schedule an appointment for a face-to-face meeting. Others must carry this stage through over the telephone.

It's probably a good idea to *think* of this stage as a face-to-face meeting, however, whether or not you actually make it in to meet the prospect. That's because the information you'll be looking for is vitally important—even though you may be asking for it only seconds after confirming more trivial details (such as whether you've reached 555-3456). Once you enter Stage Two, you must be prepared to pinpoint the facts that will allow you to make the proper recommendations to your prospect later on.

There are usually three basic questions to ask at this stage: What happened in the past? What is happening in the present? and What is forecast for the future? Before you can ask them, however, there is the question of making a smooth transition from one stage to the next. Accordingly, you will begin Stage Two by offering a brief (!) introduction to you, the company, and the product or service. You will proceed to obtain the important information about past, present, and future, adding "how" and "why" variations when this is appropriate.

Mr. Smith: Well . . . Okay, go ahead.

>   *You:* Mr. Smith, let me tell you a little bit about us. XYZ has been in business for the last twelve years, and we happen to produce the finest-quality widgets in the United States. The reason for my call today is that I'm curious about some of the specifics concerning your widget use.

> *Mr. Smith:* Okay.

>   *You:* (*Past:*) Have you worked with any widget company before?

> *Mr. Smith:* I believe we did—back in '82. We used *you* guys once.

>   *You:* How did it work out?

> *Mr. Smith:* Well, Joan, if I recall correctly the problem was one of budget limitations. We had to do some pretty serious cutting. You know how it is. Eventually we did re-establish the widget service with another vendor.

>   *You:* (*Present:*) What are you using presently?

> *Mr. Smith:* Right now we're using the Cheapo model.

>   *You:* Okay. (*Future:*) Can you tell me something, Mr. Smith? What does your discombobulating department foresee in the way of widget use over the next six months or so?

> *Mr. Smith:* Well, I was just talking to Pete Weiss over in Discombobulating this morning. He said they've just landed a new rediscombobulating project that will be taking up most of the available widget time.

Given this type of response, you might proceed by pointing out that your firm now offers the Model 77 Widget, as well as the Model 44, its lower-priced counterpart. But you do *not* ask Mr. Smith if he's ready to *buy* either of these items yet. That's closing, and we still haven't gotten there. Once you offer to show how you can solve Mr. Smith's problems and receive a positive or assenting signal in return (such as "Okay," "That sounds interesting," or "How much do those run?"), you must still work through to presentation.

Stage Three: Presentation

Up to this point, what do you know? Well, you know Mr. Smith is a qualified prospect, and you know he is interested in learning more about how your product or service can help him. That's all.

Your next step is to outline exactly how your widget will be able to solve Mr. Smith's problems. You will do this in a professional, nonconfrontational manner by focusing in on three important factors. These are *benefit, features, and proof.* Let's take a moment to define each of those terms.

The *benefit* of the widget is what Mr. Smith will get out of it. Anything that solves Mr. Smith's problem *as he defines it* (typically in terms of productivity or cost savings) is a benefit. The conversation above leads us to believe that the main problem Mr. Smith faces is managing the rediscombobulating traffic he and Pete Weiss foresee. Your widget's ability to rediscombobulate 20% faster and more accurately than anything else on the market would probably be perceived as a significant benefit. A cost savings of $10,000 over the nearest competitor would also be likely to be seen as a significant benefit. (When you're dealing with imaginary products like widgets, it's easy to offer both ends of the benefit spectrum!)

Features are the "bells and whistles" you can offer Mr. Smith. Your widget might be easy to clean. It might handle well. It might be green. All these are features. They are secondary components of the widget that do not translate into immediate benefits for the user, but are nevertheless perceived as positives.

Proof is usually testimonials or outside endorsements. A positive review of your widget in a respected industry trade magazine would be proof; so would a third-party recommendation or reference. (*Note:* In some settings, you may decide to lead with your story that provides proof, then follow up with benefit and features.)

These terms are for your use in classifying and prioritizing your presentation to the prospect. As a general rule, you will not use them in conversation with prospects. Here's what the presentation part of your call to Mr. Smith might sound like:

> *You:* Mr. Smith, I want to tell you a little bit about the Model 44, which sounds to me as though it would fit into your budget better than what you're currently using. It will help you increase production by as much as twenty percent. That's because it requires less maintenance, it's easy to clean, and it has the highest input-output rate of any widget in its class. It also happens to have been selected by *Widgets Monthly* as the top widget of 1992.

> *Mr. Smith:* Is that so. Well, it sounds intriguing, Joan, but I'm afraid I'm not the only person you're going to have to bowl over around here. We'd need to see something that shows us how the model works on the shop floor, as opposed to in the laboratory.

> *You:* Great, Mr. Smith. I should mention in passing, though, that there are a great many people who have signed on with us on the Model 44. Jon Choate over at LMN Corporation uses this model exclusively, and has told me he will

never buy another widget from anyone else as long as he's handling LMN's purchasing. For my part, I feel this product is something that could benefit your company, too.

Before you go on, reread the exchange above. What is the benefit offered? What are the features of the Model 44? What is the proof?

Stop now and review the material. Then come back and see how your answers rate.

◆　　◆　　◆

BENEFITS: Cost savings (implied, but not specified); 20% increase in production.

FEATURES: Low maintenance requirements; ease of cleaning; high input-output rate.

PROOF: Review in *Widgets Monthly*; reference from Jon Choate of LMN Corporation.

(Again, you may wish to alter the order. In many settings, it will be advisable to tell the story, explain the benefit the other person found, then sell the features.)

◆　　◆　　◆

It is during the third stage that you are most likely to encounter objections from the prospect. You can probably guess what the main weapon at your disposal is: the All-Purpose Turnaround.

You: Mr. Smith, I appreciate your hesitation about
the Model 44's (price/durability/training
wheels, whatever). But I have to tell you, your
reaction is exactly the same as Joe Brown's was,
over at ABC Company—and now he's one of
our best customers.

Naturally, you have to use a little common sense with
this method. I certainly would not advise you to employ
this technique when you are confronted with arcane or
unique objections none of your prospects has ever raised.

Later in the book, we will examine some more methods
for dealing with objections. For now, familiarize yourself
with the All-Purpose Turnaround. If you use it correctly, I
think you'll find it a very valuable tool indeed.

Stage Four: Closing

When should you try to close? The potential market
differences from product to product and industry to industry are so vast that there really is no way to give a single correct answer. The best general answer is that you should
close when you feel all the prospect's concerns and objections have been met, and when you and the prospect are in
agreement as to the theoretical advantages of going with
your product or service. (Of course, for some telemarketers,
the whole issue of "closing" *per se* is irrelevant, as their main
concern is not to finalize the sale, but rather to schedule an
appointment. We'll examine the special challenges of this
type of call a little later on in the book.)

When to try to close, then, is a complex issue. Much
easier is the question of *how* to close . . . or, more accurately,
how not to. Many salespeople cruise through the first three
stages confidently, then get a sudden case of the jitters when
they realize there's nothing left to do but try to finalize the
sale. Some sales books will advise you to pursue a "condi-

tional" or "trial" close, arguing that if you leave yourself the room to maneuver, you will be able to come back later with the genuine article and win the prospect over. I say that's a mistake. First of all, it's too adversarial. You're not out to "win over" the prospect. You want to *help* him or her. And secondly, this approach, like so many misguided pieces of advice on closing, views the final stage of the sale in a vacuum, as though it existed independently of that which has gone before. The close is the *natural next step* for both you and the prospect. Your goal is not to bring light down from the heavens where none shone before, but to take the initiative and finalize the implementation of the solutions both you and the prospect have been envisioning.

Don't hem and haw. If you've laid the proper groundwork, and if the prospect has determined that the benefits of what you have to offer are geniune, there is really no big secret about the best way to close a sale. Use the Assumptive Close. It sounds like this:

> *You:* Mr. Smith, you know what I'd like to do? I'd like to get that paperwork started today so that we can be in business next week.

Or better still:

> *You:* You know, Mr. Smith, I'd sure like to have your business. Can I write up the order?

> *You:* Well, Mr. Jones, let's write up the order. When would you want the service to start?

Even if you feel that such an approach is much too aggressive, I strongly suggest that you give it a try. I think you'll be pleasantly surprised with the results. (By the way, there's nothing at all "aggressive" about following up on mutually acknowledged interest on the part of your prospect.)

Make the assumption that the sale will close. Ask for the sale in terms that the prospect will find non-threatening. Try to initiate the paperwork. It's that simple.

Will you get shot down? Sometimes. But what's the alternative? You can't keep babbling about how wonderful your widgets are. Mr. Smith has heard that already. Ask for the business. Then stop talking and see what kind of answer comes back.

I work with a lot of companies, and I see thousands of salespeople every year. Not infrequently, I'm asked to give "seminars on how to improve closing techniques" to various groups. Do you know what I say? I tell them, "I can't offer you that seminar."

And I really can't. Looking at closing as an independent entity, as a component separate from the rest of the sales cycle, really is the biggest part of the problem! Therefore, it's pointless for me to come in and do one single day specifically targeted toward improving closing ratios. It's like asking how to improve your bathroom scale so that you'll lose weight when you step on it. It's an attractive idea, but there are a couple of key stages to the process that need to be dealt with first.

Believe me, if I *could* honestly offer people pointers on simply "improving closing techniques," without dealing in detail with what precedes the closing attempt, I certainly would. But I can't. And nobody else can, either.

"Well," you may find yourself wondering, "what happens if the straight assumptive close doesn't work? What are you supposed to do then?" There are a couple of avenues I'd suggest for dealing with situations where you feel the groundwork really has been laid properly, but you're still having trouble getting the prospect to commit to a program or product of genuine benefit to him or her.

First, you can suggest a scaled back or less expensive version of what you were offering. I call that the Downscale Model Response. Or you could use the Future Response, in which you point out that your real aim is to help the prospect avoid some unpleasant development on your end over which you have no control (a price hike, for instance, or a tightening of credit terms). You can offer the Incentive Response, in which you give a bonus of some kind—a free service contract, say—as a premium for agreeing to sign on. (Check with your sales manager before offering anything of this kind, however.) Finally, you can use the Endorsement Response, in which you suggest a three-party conference call that allows your prospect to hear from a happy customer who's in love with what you have to offer. (Of course, you must clear such referrals through the third party ahead of time. You won't get far with a prospect by surprising your "happy" customer at five minutes to five on deadline day.)

PART II

CUSTOMIZING YOUR APPROACH

CHAPTER SIX

CRAFTING YOUR MESSAGE

All that stuff about the development of the sales cycle is fine. But what, exactly, are you supposed to *say*?

As you know by now, I'm on record against the use of a script as a transcript to be read verbatim to (at!) the prospect. However, the fact that a script can be misused is not an indictment against its proper use.

The key is to think of your script as the means by which you communicate your message, and not the message itself. That means you're going to feel free to improvise when occasion demands, and you're going to alter your approach depending on your read of how the prospect is reacting to your proposals.

In this chapter, we'll look at the best ways for you to develop your script. We'll assume that your goal is to close the sale by phone. (You can easily make your own adjustments to suit your needs for other calls. Closing by phone is certainly the most difficult objective!)

Your Own Approach

You should develop your own personal telemarketing script— or, at the very least, adapt an existing one to your

71

strengths. As a side note, let me say that I'm extremely skeptical of anyone who tries to compose a "one-size-fits-all" script that is meant for use by an entire department. One size really can't fit all, at least not in this case. There are too many variables in play, too many key differences among good salespeople. As we've seen, the key to quickly developing "top of the mind awareness" in dealing with your prospect is to build and project a competent professional image that sets you apart from the rest of the pack. Trying to do that with words that were written by someone else and for "sales reps in general" is like trying to beat the heavyweight champion with your hands tied behind your back. The plan should be designed around you, not the other way around. Put the message into your words.

Following is a list of guidelines and suggestions on how you can go about doing just that.

The Opening Statement

Does this sound familiar?

> "Hi, have I reached Mr. Jones? I have? Great! That's super, Mr. Jones! That is supergreat! Mr. Jones, if I could get you a two-billion dollar return on a fifty-five cent investment, would you be interested?"

What on earth are you supposed to say to someone who interrupts your dinner to ask you a question like that?

There's been a great deal of talk in recent years about the necessity of coming up with a "can't-miss grabber" of an opening statement, one that will really stop the prospect in his or her tracks. The result: ridiculous, self-defeating "grabbers" that zoom so far beyond the horizon that they fail to grab anyone. The example I've used above is an exaggeration of the trend—but not by much.

We've pushed this "grabber" idea a little too far, I think. Yes, you must certainly come up with a compelling beginning to your pitch. But no, you do not have to stretch your own credibility to the breaking point in the first ten seconds of the conversation. You're a professional, and professionals don't tell tall tales. Remember, you're after a career, not a sale. You're trying to build a network of contacts and a satisfied customer base, not ambush the unprepared and credulous.

Neither, for that matter, is your aim to turn off qualified prospects, You need to get important information from the people you talk to, and they're certainly not going to feel comfortable giving it to you if they equate your call with a slap across the face. Some telemarketers in the financial field use this upstart approach:

> Good morning, Mr. Smith. Do you have ten thousand dollars to invest?

Good lord! If someone asked you that at a party, you'd turn on your heel and walk away! Even if you were forgiving enough to answer with something resembling truthfulness, the odds are that you *wouldn't* tell the caller about the stock fund you control, or about any of a hundred other factors that might affect the way the sales call should proceed. What a handicap that is for a telemarketer!

Start calmly. Start professionally. Say:

> "Good morning (or afternoon), Mr. Smith. This is Julia Gayle; I'm with Essex Manufacturing, and I'm calling from Boston. How are you today?"

This approach does a number of important things.

First, notice that it uses the prospect's name. You may already know that the use of a person's name is one of the most dependable ways to win attention during the sales call. But don't overdo it! Repeating the prospect's name endlessly shows that you are presumptuous.

In addition, you will notice that you identify yourself almost immediately in the opening sentences I've given. You say who you are, what company you work for, and where you're calling from. What's more, you'll extend a "verbal handshake" ("How are you today?") that allows the prospect to participate in the conversation. All of this builds credibility, an essential component in professional telemarketing work.

I strongly suggest that you use both your first and last names. Omitting the first name ("Ms. Gayle") makes you sound like you run a collection agency. Omitting the last name ("Julia") is too chummy for a relationship that is not yet one minute old. If you have problems about using your real name because of personal security issues, I suggest that you adopt a pseudonym for your phone work—and stick to it.

After identifying yourself, you'll want to give the reason for your call.

> "The reason I'm calling you today is that my company has asked me to reach out to homeowners in the Swansea area to tell them about some of the new products and services we're offering."

> "The reason I'm calling you today is that my firm is reaching out to people in the widget business to tell them about some of the things we do."

Such an approach may seem modest or understated if you're used to high-voltage "grabber" techniques, but the truth is the opening I've just described is far more effective. If you deliver the phrases sincerely and openly, with no air of sham or suspicious speed, you will be building the foundation of a relationship with your prospect. Right away, you will have distinguished yourself from the flim-flam artists, because you will have said who you are, what firm you represent, and what you do. The prospect will be able to sense that you are not trying to get away with anything, and the natural distrust will begin to ease.

Of course, you're only beginning the process now. You can't expect the prospect to hear your sincerity and say, "Sign me up." There are probably a number of obstacles you must still overcome. But how much better positioned you are to cross them than if you had attempted to "grab" your prospect by promising everything!

The Transition to Information Gathering

Continue by telling the prospect exactly where you'd like the conversation to go. It should be second nature to you by now to begin the interviewing or information gathering portion of the call. But be careful. Don't rush. Be calm, persistent, and confident. If the prospect wants to interrupt, back off and listen. *Don't worry* about what you'll say if the prospect has an objection. Remember that the All-Purpose Turnaround will cover many, many, of these concerns.

Let's take a look at a few of the many, many ways you could manage the transition.

> "The reason I'm calling you, Mr. Smith, is that my company's asked me to tell you about our new insurance offer, which many of the homeowners here in the Kansas City area have found can save them money. I wanted to check in with you today to get some information so that I can determine whether or not our product might be of use to you. Is that all right?"

"Mr. Smith, you might already be familiar with our firm; ABC Widgets has been in business since 1966. I was calling today to see if I could ask a couple of quick questions to determine whether we might be able to help you increase your productivity. Have you got a moment for that?"

"XYZ Temporary Agency just completed a major project in your area, Mr. Smith. The reason I had wanted to give you a call today was to ask you a few quick questions that will help me find out if there might be a good match between our firm and yours. How does that sound to you?"

These are *not* magic words guaranteed to work in every sales situation, but rough guidelines intended for your use as you develop your own customized outline. Don't let the words stop you. It is in this part of the script, the transition to information gathering, that you can move beyond the hard-and-fast principles I've outlined for the structuring of your opening, and really let your own creativity come into play. In the end, you will be the best judge of what your prospects will react positively to—and what you will be comfortable saying.

However you decide to put your message together, I strongly advise you to maintain a forthright, open approach with the prospect. The truth cannot be changed. If your aim is to learn about the prospect's needs, there is nothing to be gained by trying to weasel the information out a little at a time. Your best bet is always to tell the prospect exactly what you are doing, as you are doing it. By putting all the cards on the table, by stating openly and honestly that you're calling to get more information from the prospect about how you might be able to help him or her, you will earn a significant measure of respect. And you will stand out from the legions of other telemarketers who sound as though they're hoping to close the present sale, then catch the midnight train out of town as soon as they get the check.

Before we move on, I want to note once again that you can expect to hear an objection or two at this stage. We've already discussed the use of the All-Purpose Turnaround. A full examination of some other techniques for turning around objections will come later.

For now, let's take a good look at what you *shouldn't* do in response to a prospect's objections.

> *You:* Mr. Smith, I'd like to ask you a couple of very quick questions about how we can best serve your home insurance needs if I may. Is that all right?

> *Mr. Smith:* No. We already have a policy. I'm not interested.

> *You:* Well, Mr. Smith, I happen to know that ABC Insurance can save you a lot of money over what you're presently using.

or:

> *You:* Well, Mr. Smith, I'm not sure I understand you there. Are you saying you're not interested in saving money?

or:

> *You:* Well, Mr. Smith, how can you be sure that policy is right for you?

Stop and think for a moment. How would *you* react to the challenging, partnership-destroying questions you just read?

You, as a prospect, probably hear these kinds of comebacks when you're approached by a telemarketer. Be honest. Don't they drive you nuts? Don't they make you want to scream back something equally combative? "So I'm stupid. So I already *bought* the policy. That's life. Sue me for throwing my own money down the tubes." "No. I'm brain damaged. I'm not interested in saving money. But thanks for asking." "I'm sure that policy is right for me because I asked my mommy about it this morning,and she said it was okay."

But generally, you probably don't do that. (Well, maybe if you've had a particularly rough day . . . .) Generally, what you probably do is say something like, "Sorry, I'm really not interested." And you hang up.

That is what awaits *you* when you dig in your heels against the prospect. What on earth are you going to gain by subjecting the prospect to cross-examination? You don't want to wage a war of wits against this person. You want to build bridges.

Maintain a positive, upbeat, professional attitude even—*especially*—in the face of objections, and, for now, just stick with the All-Purpose Turnaround whenever you can.

You: Mr. Smith, I'd like to ask you a couple of very quick questions about how we can best serve your home insurance needs if I may. Is that all right?

Mr. Smith: No. We already have a policy. I'm not interested.

You: You know, I certainly realize how you might feel that way, Mr. Smith, because that's exactly what most of my customers said before they signed on with us. But once we had a chance to talk things over, they went with us and, on average, realized a 20% savings over their current insurer. What I'd like to do now is take just a minute of your time to see if there's the possibility we could save you some money, too. Is that all right?

What have you done? You've made it clear that the prospect's reaction is valid. (Other people just like him have reacted in the same way.) Perhaps most important, you've sent the prospect a message that *that reaction is okay*. You're used to it. You're a professional. You know this field. Something like the issue Mr. Smith has raised comes up all the time in your line of work, and you know how to deal with it without destroying anyone's self-image. You will also be sending the underlying message that you *want* the prospect to tell you about such issues, because it's by learning more about that prospect's circumstances that you will ultimately be able to do your job.

By contrast, the message the cross-examiners send is: "Your reaction is invalid, and I don't want to hear it. The way you are viewing your situation is totally wrong-headed—and, what's more, it annoys the hell out of me to have to listen to it." Now, who's going to buy based on a message like that?

I think you will be amazed how many supposedly "tough" prospects will give you the chance to proceed once you present things to them in the way I've suggested. I'm not saying this method works all the time; nothing works all the time. But I will promise you that you will convert *more* initial objections by taking the reasoned, sober, professional approach I've just outlined than you will by bashing the prospect over the head with confrontational questions designed to prove he or she is wrong and you are right.

Information Gathering

" Well . . . okay."

When you hear something like this in response to your request to ask the prospect a few questions, you will know that it is time to move on to the interviewing stage of your script. *Do not* make the mistake of trying to move ahead to this stage if you have not received a clear signal of assent. To be sure, that assent may be couched in terms of doubt or impatience: "I'm really busy right now/It's probably too expensive, but . . . ." That's okay. Sometimes prospects need to establish a kind of "escape hatch" before they enter into *any* discussion with you about the product or service. Let them. But do not attempt to pressure the prospect into entering this stage with you; that will backfire just about every time. (By the way, I consider a polite pause in the conversation to allow you to proceed to be a positive sign. What I'm warning you against doing is wasting your time with people who are overtly hostile to your message and committed to staying that way.)

Only you can structure the particular questions of the interviewing stage. After all, you know the specifics of your company, product or service, and market far better than I do. But there are a few guidelines I'm going to suggest you follow.

As we saw earlier, your questions should concern themselves with the prospect's past history with regard to using your type of product or service, the present situation, and the prospects for the future. You should add appropriate "how" and "why" questions, as well: Why did you stop the service? How does your present service handle (area of your firm's strength)?

In addition, you're best advised to stay away from questions of the "yes-or-no" variety. Exchanges like the following probably won't do your cause much good.

> *You:* Mr. Smith, are you happy with your present set of windows?

Mr. Smith. Yes.

It's far better to leave a little gray area. When you enter into this stage, consider your objective to be to make the prospect actually stop to think about the areas in which your firm can offer tangible solutions. Paint a picture. Ask an "example" question.

> *You:* Mr. Smith, a lot of the people I've been talking to find that their windows seem to present no obvious problems at a glance, but that their homes have strange drafts and breezes at night. Have you noticed anything like that?

Note, too, that Mr. Smith can respond to this question in the way you want him to *without committing himself to your service.* Pressure is for cookers, not for prospects! People need to be able to enter into a dialogue with you without feeling that you're preparing to pounce on them if they respond in the way you hope. In the first example, the one with the "yes-or-no" question, the prospect almost certainly knows that to answer "No" is to invite you to launch another assault. He may even be afraid that if he answers "No," you will enroll him right there and send him a bill!

You may think that sounds far-fetched, but today's prospects have to put up with a lot of guff that's not too far removed from such techniques. A major long-distance service came under serious media scrutiny and may face hefty fines for the "innovative" practices of its aggressive telemarketers. These practices included listing as "sales" those prospects who hung up on the telemarketers without actually saying that they weren't interested in the service. The company dutifully switched these people over and sent them bills!

The last thing you want is to be confused with telemarketers like that. Keep it light and nonthreatening. Structure your questions in such a way that they leave the prospect plenty of breathing room.

Ask a total of three to five questions. Four tends to be the best number, but your product or service may require something different. However many questions you choose, don't drag the process out. At the conclusion of your questioning, you may feel it is appropriate to conclude this stage by saying something along the following lines.

> *You:* Well, Mr. Smith, based on the information you've given me, I think we can help you.

In effect, you say to the prospect: I did the work here. I've taken the trouble to find out some of the key facts, and I can tell you that you fit the profile. I've helped a lot of people like you, and I think you'll benefit from listening to what I have to say.

Of course, if you determine that the person does *not* fit your profile, you should thank him or her for the time spent and move on to your next call. Don't send out information just for the (false) sense of accomplishment. Don't try to convince someone on welfare to subscribe to your investment letter. Don't get worked up trying to sell car insurance to a person whose sole means of transportation for the past twenty years has been a 1972 Schwinn. Don't waste valuable time trying to turn a rock-hard "no" into a "yes." Move on.

The Presentation Stage

Once you have built a bridge of trust between yourself and the project, you will be in a good position to make a presentation. During this presention, you will set out specifically how you want to help the prospect solve the problem you have identified together.

As we saw in an earlier part of the book, your focus should be on benefit, features, and proof. Do not draw your presentation out; keep it short enough for the prospect to follow easily. In general, you will probably find it does your cause more harm than good to use lots of facts, figures, and technical jargon. Keep things simple if you can. (Of course, the exception to this is when you are selling to someone with a technical background. In this case, you will probably have to supply all the details, but do so in such a way as to allow the prospect to feel the information flow is manageable. Do not rush ahead if one of your points seems not to have sunk in.)

Your presentation may sound something like this.

> *You:* Mr. Smith, the reason I ask you all this is that we've been behind a very successful new grocery service in your area that can save you between fifteen and twenty percent. ExpressShop does the comparison shopping for you on key items by visiting multiple stores over the course of a day. When you specify, we'll retain the sizes and brands you request, so you probably won't notice any difference in your cupboard. And we're very easy to use; you just check off the items you desire from our master list and make your preferences known. It takes about ten minutes. If I could add one more thing, Mr. Smith, let me point out that *Metro Shopper Weekly* called our service "the best thing to happen to shoppers since double coupons" in the February 14th issue. Now, given what you've told me today, I think our service could be right for you.

Here's an instance where we told the story (gave the proof) first, then went into the specific benefits of the service, and finally focused on the features.

To give yourself some more practice, why don't you review the presentation above and see if you can identify the benefit, the features, and the proof. Compare your answers to those that follow.

◆   ◆   ◆

BENEFIT: Average 20% savings on grocery bills

FEATURES: Ability to retain favorite brands; ease and speed of selection.

PROOF: Favorable mention in *Metro Shopper Weekly*.

◆   ◆   ◆

Make sure your presentation paints a picture. Obviously, you have to discuss the product, but you want to be sure you highlight the benefits, and use the features and proof as supporting points. It is a common error for salespeople (those selling by phone as well as those working in a face-to-face environment) to focus on the elements they feel set them apart from the competition—styling, service contracts, delivery schedules, and so on—when these are not the main objective of the prospect in considering a purchase. Your aim is to *get the prospect to envision the benefit as though it were already in effect*. That's painting a picture. The rest should follow naturally.

Remember, on the telephone, the prospect is concentrating less on you and more on your message. That means you're in a much better position to help the prospect form a mental image of your product or service benefit than the salesperson who must make an in-person presentation.

Consider incorporating something like the following into your presentation.

> *You:* Mr. Smith, my guess is that you, like the other people I've spoken to, probably don't list shoveling out your driveway as your favorite thing to do after a major snowstorm. It's hard work, and for some people it's even dangerous. But let's face it, a blocked-up driveway is inconvenient. Somehow, we all have to get dug out. That's where we come in. ABC ShovelTruck guarantees you complete freedom of movement by six-thirty a.m., no matter what—or we'll double your money back. There's no sweating and straining, no getting up at the crack of dawn, and no shivering, either. You get up— your driveway's clear.

The Close

The close has already been covered in detail in the previous chapter. Just as a reminder, however, I'll note that your close should arise directly and naturally from the work you do in the previous three stages, and it should not be watered down or qualified in any way. When you have determined that the time has come to try to close the sale, come right out and ask for the business in a confident, nonagressive manner.

In a telemarketing environment, the close often (but not always) immediately follows the presentation. Your requirements may, of course, be different, but the scenario below, which links the close directly to the presentation, can serve as a good all-purpose model.

> *You:* Mr. Smith, given what you've said to me just now, I think I should tell you a little bit about

the Model 44 widget. It sounds to me as though it would fit into your budget better than what you're currently using. The Model 44 will help you increase production by as much as twenty percent. That's because it requires less maintenance, it's easy to clean, and it has the highest input-output rate of any widget in its class. It also happens to have been selected by *Widgets Monthly* as the top widget of 1992. With all that in mind, Mr. Smith, what I'd like to do now is get the paperwork going so we can schedule a time for our service people to come over to your place and hook you up with a new Model 44. Okay?

A Variation on the Standard Script

Consider using the following variation if you are telemarketing to follow up any kind of qualified mailing that does (or may do) some of the qualifying and presentation for you. The technique is particularly effective if you are calling people who have been sent direct-marketing pieces but have not responded to them.

You: Good evening, Mr. Jones, this is Julia Gayle calling from ABC Widget out in North Attleboro, Massachusetts. How are you tonight?

Mr. Smith: Very well, thanks.

You: Mr. Smith, I was just wondering if you'd received our recent mailing—the big yellow envelope with the red stripe along one side. Do you recall?

Mr. Smith: [Any response.]

You: Okay, well I'll note that on this end. I'd like to tell you my reason for calling tonight if I could:

We got such a great response to that mailing that ABC has asked me to reach out to some of the area people who have used widgets in the past. I don't know if you're familiar with our widget rediscombobulating program or not, Mr. Smith, but it can save you up to fifteen percent on your annual widget bills. We did just that for a family in Middleton; they estimate their annual savings at fifteen hundred dollars. Another family over in Boxford did even better. They tell us they saved two thousand dollars last year.

The structure is as follows: opening, explanation of reason for call (with the mailing serving as a buffer of sorts), and two success stories. You can then proceed to field any questions that arise, bearing in mind the applicability of the All-Purpose Turnaround, and eventually proceed to either close the sale or set an appointment, depending on the type of call you are making.

There are a number of important assumptions underlying this approach that you must be aware of before attempting to use it. You must be sure that:

♦ The mailing was directed at a good-quality list of prospects. A mailing to "the general public" will not serve you in good stead if you attempt to use this technique. There must be some level of qualification to the list you will be calling.

♦ You have in fact gotten a good response to the mailing.

♦ You have secured the formal or informal permissions of the people or companies whose success stories you will be citing. (This is a good rule to follow in employing any kind of endorsement.)

Helpful Hints

Here are some general tips that will help you make your script something the prospect will want to react to positively.

1. Be sincere. Remember, your goal is to see if you can *help* the prospect. You should tell the prospect that, but it should be evident from the attitude that accompanies every syllable that comes out of your mouth. Do not try to ram the call down the prospect's throat, and do not adopt a style that is foreign to you. Let your own personality be the driving force of the call.

2. Slow down when you speak. Give the person time to react to you and to your message. After all, you're calling the prospect away from some other matter he or she is likely to consider, at least at first, more pressing than talking to you. Let the potential benefits of what you are discussing be crystal clear. If you rush through the script, you risk alienating the prospect by making your message difficult or impossible to make out.

3. Keep your script in front of you for purposes of reference. Not to read from verbatim, mind you, but to appeal to in case the progression or tempo of the call shifts suddenly. A script is preparation, not a set of handcuffs. Use it as such.

4. Listen, listen, listen. I've touched on this point elsewhere, but it bears repeating. If the prospect goes to the trouble of saying something, you must go to the trouble to listen to it and understand it *from the prospect's point of view*. I know of salespeople who write the word "LISTEN" in

large letters on a three-by-five card, then post it where they can see it whenever they make calls. It's an approach worth considering.

5. Mentally review your calls after you've made them. Where could you have reacted more effectively to a prospect's concern or problem? Was there a point at which you tried to move the prospect along too soon? Do you find yourself hemming and hawing when it comes time to close? Keep a watchful eye out for signs of any of these problems, and follow the advice from earlier sections of this book in overcoming them.

6. Don't speak in code. If you let technical jargon or industry doubletalk slip into your script, you will undercut your sales efforts. Make sure that everything you say will be easily understood by the average person. (On the other hand, if your *prospect* starts using technical terms in reaction to you, you should definitely be able to respond in kind.)

7. Monitor and record in a journal the common patterns of your calls. After a while, you will find that certain questions, reactions, and obstacles can be expected over the long term with regard to your product or service. I can't write them down here, because I don't work in the same area you do. (Unless, of course, you're a sales trainer, in which case you probably don't need this book in the first place.) You *should* write down the common twists and turns of your calls. By recording them in a notebook, you'll be able to note important signals, nip small problems in the bud before they become big problems, and act on opportunities early.

CHAPTER SEVEN

OBJECTIONS

Most objections are *opportunities waiting to be taken advantage of.*

When a prospect goes to the trouble of telling you exactly what his or her problem is—cost, performance, competition, schedules, whatever—you are in a better position with that person than you were before you knew the details. You now have a better idea of what hurdles lie ahead of you. Most important, you know what the problem looks like *to the prospect.* And it is always in those terms that you should try to resolve the problem.

Before we get into specifics, I want to preface the techniques you'll learn about in this chapter by saying that there really is no such thing as a final, unconditional, impossible-to-respond-to objection. You may think there is, but there really isn't. The closest any salesperson can ever come to that kind of objection is the scenario in which the prospect makes it clear that "no purchase is going to be made at this point in time."

The key words there are, "at this point in time."

Fine. No sale at this point in time. That takes care of right now. But right now is *not* all you're interested in. Because you're a professional salesperson, you can, if you wish, hold on to that prospect's name. And three to six months from now, you can approach that prospect again to see if he or she is interested in talking to you. A lot can change in three to six months. Your prospect's whole life could be turned upside down. That tight budget problem may well be history.

I say this not just to encourage you to follow up on rejections in the long term (although it is an excellent practice that will definitely win you sales); I say it to bring the whole issue of objections into the proper perspective. Salespeople are usually *terrified* of getting shot down by the prospect. That's unnecessary and counterproductive. We'll learn in this chapter about some very effective techniques you can use to deal with the objections you get—and if they don't work, that's really no big deal. You've added a name to your long-term prospect list. You're now free to move on to someone else.

Anytime, Anywhere

There's no point in the sales cycle at which the prospect can be depended upon to consistently offer up all of his or her objections. It can happen at any point in your call, and it can happen without warning.

Every objection can be broken down into one of the a number of basic types. We'll be examining them shortly. My bet is that, within those types, there are specific objections associated with your firm's product or service that you can be more prepared for than you are. If you get anything out of this chapter, it should be that once you hear objection "X" for the fiftieth time, you should be more prepared to deal with it, and have a better idea of what works and what doesn't, than you did the first time you heard it.

Of course, we've already examined one very important tool for overcoming objections. Let's look at it in a little more detail right now.

The All-Purpose Turnaround Revisited

With the All-Purpose Turnaround, you basically tell the prospect that you've heard his or her objection before from people who ended up becoming your customers. You may feel comfortable using the All-Purpose Turnaround "straight," or you may want to introduce it with the "Can-I-ask-a-question" technique:

> *You:* What we're doing today is giving area car-owners the chance to take a look at our program in a little more detail. I'd like to stop by to tell you about some of the things we've been . . .
>
> *Mr. Smith:* Let me stop you right there, Joan. I'm very happy with what I have right now.
>
> *You:* Well, Mr. Smith, can I ask you one question?
>
> *Mr. Smith:* Sure.
>
> *You:* Just out of curiosity, how are you presently meeting your auto widget needs?

This quick incursion into the information gathering stage will almost always be enough to get the prospect to focus on the subject at hand—widget use—rather than the problem of how best to get you off the phone. Because the person has made a negative statement in suggesting that it isn't necessary for the two of you to get together, you can often get a counterbalancing positive (that is, a reasonable answer) in response to your subsequent question. You can then follow up with the All-Purpose Turnaround.

> *Mr. Smith:* We're using Brand X.
>
> *You:* You know, Mr. Smith, it's interesting that you should say that; many of my former customers used Brand X . . .

This should be enough for you to get the conversation back on track.

A variation on this is to ask *neutral, risk-free* yes-or-no questions and use the prospect's response to guide the conversation back into first gear.

Mr. Smith: Let me stop you right there, Joan. I'm very happy with what I have right now.

You: Well, Mr. Smith, can I ask you one question?

Mr. Smith: Sure.

You: Are you using the Model 4000 widget in your home?

Mr. Smith: (Any yes-or-no response.)

You: [In response to "yes" answer:] The reason I ask is that a lot of the Model 4000 users responded in just the way you just did before they found that our Model Nine delivers the same results at a fraction of the cost . . .

You: [In response to "no" answer:] The reason I ask is that a good portion of our customers are those who don't require the power of the Model 4000. A good many of them had just the same reaction you did before they had the chance to look at our Model Two, which is an affordable low-end alternative that provides . . .

With any luck, you will be able to proceed from here into the information gathering stage. Remember, your goal is not to badger the prospect, but to get him or her focused on ways you can help to solve a problem.

Now that we've seen some of the variations you can use with the All-Purpose Turnaround, let's move on to a more in-depth look at how salespeople deal with objections.

Catch!

How do you think you reacted as a little child the first time your mother or father threw a ball your way?

Like most of us would have as children, you probably just ducked, hoping to protect yourself. My bet is that it wasn't until the third, fourth, or fifth time that you finally realized they were throwing the ball to you, not at you, and attempted to catch the ball.

Maybe after your first few attempts at trying to catch the ball, you learned that by putting your arms up in a certain position, you could knock the ball down and make it land in front of you. And perhaps from there you learned that, with a little more practice, you could actually catch it and throw it back.

What we've just described is exactly the progression most salespeople go through when they begin trying to manage objections. Most of them, in the early stages, simply duck for cover, trying to protect themselves. They don't try to "catch" the objection, meet it, and return the dialogue to the prospect. They assume the prospect is trying to knock them down, attack them, and the exchanges quickly become polarized. Unnecessary conflicts arise. That, obviously, is not the environment in which you want to do business as a professional telemarketer. Too many telemarketers are taken by surprise when it comes to objections. Too many think the prospect is trying to pick a fight—rather than find a solution to a problem. Don't become one of them. Become a professional problem-solver.

The Underlying Language of the Objection

It is more important to understand where an objection comes from than it is to document the actual words used to express it. Words, by themselves, often don't give you all the information you need. In an objection (as in any other form of communication) the context is all-important. If I were to ask "How *old* are you," emphasizing the word "old," you would get one message. Quite a different signal would come through, however, if put the accent on the final word and asked "How old are *you?*"

Variations in meaning accompany most of the standard objections. There's nothing I'd like more to be able to tell you, "When they say this, it always means thus-and-so, and it always comes at this point in the presentation, and here's how you turn it around." But telemarketing is a little more subtle than that. Fortunately, there is an approach you can take that's proven very effective for many, many salespeople. It's a three-step system that helps you work with the prospects you encounter, not against them.

The first step is to identify the objection. The second is to validate it. The third is to resolve it.

That may sound like a tall order, but it is easier than you think. Your mental attitude—how you handle the split-second following the prospect's objection—is probably the single most important factor in determining your success in dealing effectively with the prospect's concerns. The way you respond in that split-second will determine whether or not you get a clear picture of what you're up against.

Let's make one thing clear from the outset. When you hear an objection, your first mental reaction should be to identify it. Not to get defensive or to argue about whether or not the prospect is "wrong." Focusing on "right" and "wrong" in this context is pointless. Your objective is to work with someone, not win arguments.

To gain speed and proficiency in the crucial business of identification, review the main categories below. Doing so will probably add quite a bit to your confidence level.

The Main Types of Objections

In the *stall*, the prospect tries to sidestep your efforts by postponing any decision that will move the sales cycle forward.

In the *hidden objection*, the prospect is saying one thing but acting on a set of circumstances that's quite different.

In the *hard objection*, the prospect has a good reason to believe your product or service is unnecessary, inappropriate, too expensive, or a combination of all three.

In the *easy objection*, the prospect shows evidence of genuine interest in your product or service, but offers up a technicality that stands in the way—usually one you can overcome without much difficulty. In the *reassurance request*, the prospect has trepidations about committing to you because he or she wants to see further proof of credibility from you.

Finally, in the *doubt and fear objection*, the prospect won't or can't make the decision on the issue at hand, and is unwilling to refer you to the proper person.

Of course, such labels are useful only up to a point. You can get the exact same words coming out of someone's mouth in two different situations, but the meaning can be utterly different.

If you're at the very early stages of the sale, prospecting, let's say, and the person on the other end of the line says, "Gee, let me stop you, we have no interest whatsoever in that," then you're getting one message. The person is under the impression that your product or service isn't useful. But if you're heading toward the close during your third call, having gone through extensive prospecting, interviewing, and presentation sessions, and your prospect suddenly says, "Gee, let me stop you, we have no interest whatsoever in that," then something very different has happened. Specifically, you've just learned that there's probably a problem with your interviewing skills. Either that, or you've got a prospect who's not being honest with you—in which case it's a good bet you're dealing with a problem that has not been resolved yet from the prospect's point of view.

The second step is to validate the objection. In essence, you do this by repeating the prospect's objection back to

him or her. Some telemarketers find this quite difficult—
they may feel that repeating the objection will solidify it in
the prospect's mind, or that it will show that the salesperson
is "wrong." Again, keep in mind that "right" and "wrong"
are not what matters at this stage.

After all, the objection is your prospect's reality. It is all
you have to work with. It's *already* been solidified in the
prospect's mind, otherwise the prospect wouldn't have said
it in the first place. Your only alternative is to show the prospect you're listening by repeating the perceived problem.

What good is an exchange like this going to do you?

> *Prospect:* You know what? We already have widgets that
> work just fine.
>
> *You:* No, wait, these are better, it's a brand new
> model. Just listen.

Really, aren't you just engaging in something like this?

> *Prospect:* You know what? We already have widgets that
> work just fine.
>
> *You:* What are you interrupting me for? This is an en-
> tirely different type of product, you fool; it's
> even better than what you've got now. Now be
> quiet and let me finish.

Don't do it. Don't send those kinds of signals. They lose
sales. Instead, repeat the prospect's objection, then reassure
the prospect that you can overcome the obstacle in such a
way that will make the prospect's business run more effectively or more profitably.

Of course, the third step is resolving the problem that's
been presented to you. That must be your focus, because
that's the prospect's focus.

Here's how it all might sound:

Mr. Smith: You know what? We already have widgets that work just fine.

    You: (Validate/Solve:) Oh, okay, so you have a widget service now? Well, I'll tell you, Mr. Smith, that's something I've heard from a lot of people, including many of the clients we've been working with to improve their effectiveness in this area. Their feeling on it, eventually, was that our results really spoke for themselves.

Isn't that a more relaxed, professional approach? Wouldn't you feel justified in continuing a conversation with someone who said that to you, whether or not you had widgets? Wouldn't it seem worth your while to at least hear what the person had to say?

At this point, you'll probably be in a much better position to pick up where you left off. But don't be over-hasty in doing so. If the problem has not been solved to the prospect's satisfaction, it's pointless to try to move on. Stay with your prospect, and work things out at his or her pace, not yours.

Identify the objection, preferably in such a way that you understand which of the six main categories it falls into; *acknowledge the validity* of the objection by repeating it to the prospect; do your best to resolve the problem that's been put in front of you by the prospect—and remember to use the basic turnaround technique.

The Heart of the Matter

Here are the basic guidelines to follow once you have determined the type of objection you are facing.

When the Prospect Tries to Stall

The best approach here is usually to offer a specific timetable for further action on the matter. This will not only leave you with a clear view of your next step, but also help to smoke out those who are hesitant to tell you they aren't seriously interested.

When the Prospect Says the Product or Service Costs Too Much

You usually have two options: You can discuss the advantages of a lower-priced version, or you can pro-rate the costs to place the issue in the proper perspective. To follow the second course, point out that the Model Nine will end up costing only a few cents a day over the course of a year. A related approach to pro-rating is to compare your price to that of a competitor or to the "cost" of continuing to do business without the product or service.

When the Prospect is Vague

You may get an "objection" that's intricate or unclear, leaving you with no idea of how to proceed. In these cases, it's generally best to come out and ask the client where the problem is. See the section on "Taking Responsibility" later in this chapter.

When You Are Faced With a Very Difficult Objection

As you might imagine, some objections are tougher than others. It will be very difficult indeed to turn around an objection like this:

Prospect: You know what? I just picked up one of your competitor's products last week, the Smith Model Six Widget. I got it for nothing; my brother works for Smith.

File it under "long-term possibilities." Call back in three to six months to see if anything has changed. Perhaps that unpleasant brother-in-law will have been laid off by your topheavy competitor.

It is worth noting that there are many difficult objections you should *not* give up on. Many salespeople are frustrated by objections of the "we-already-have-that" variety. In some cases, you will be able to alter the All-Purpose Turnaround to help you overcome that frustrating response.

Mr. Smith: We already have that. We're all set, thanks.

> *You:* You know, Mr. Smith, a lot of my customers once told me the same thing before they had the chance to see how what we do could complement their existing service.

Now, obviously, if you're selling house painting services, and you're talking to a homeowner who just had his house painted last week, this approach isn't going to do much for you. If, on the other hand, you're dealing with products or services that traditionally do have some potential for overlap—insurance comes to mind—it may be worth a try.

When the Prospect Focuses on a Minor Detail You Can Easily Address

Many objections are simply questions about your product or service phrased as reasons likely to block a purchase decision. Remember to remind the prospect, wherever appropriate, how "other people said exactly the same thing."

Mr. Smith: We like the color green here at our company, and all the widgets I've seen have been blue.

> *You:* Actually, that's no problem, Mr. Prospect. A lot of our customers prefer green widgets—that's why we've come out with seventeen different shades of green on the A-43.

When the Prospect Needs Reassurance or Seems to Be Doubtful about Referring You to the Ultimate Decision-Maker

Point out that other customers have gone through exactly the same stages before signing on with you. Tell one or two real-life stories that illustrate your success in overcoming the problems the prospect foresees. For those who seem to have difficulty with the very act of choosing a course of action—any course of action—take a hint from AT&T and make sure your supporting anecdotes illustrate why you're "the right choice" in an often confusing marketplace.

Taking Sincere Responsibility

If all else fails, try this.

> *You:* Mr. Smith, I have to tell you something. I am genuinely surprised to hear you say that you don't want to go along with our service, and I'll tell you why. I've been with this firm for such-and-such number of years, and I've talked to a lot of people about what we do. My feedback from over such-and-such number of customers has been very clear: they feel that we offer the best widgets, with the best site customization, at the best price available on the market today. Period. And when you've seen as many bad widget situations turned into good ones as I have, you get a real sense for the quality of your product. So I can only as-

sume, Mr. Smith, that the only reason you would decide against us on this is that *I* did something wrong, left something out, or threw things off track during my presentation just now. I'd really hate to have that happen, so I'd like to ask you to tell me where I slipped up today.

Wow! What do you suppose the prospect is going to say to something like that?

I'll tell you one thing. Assuming that it is delivered from the heart and with the requisite believability, Mr. Smith certainly is not going to respond to a request of this kind with a blithe, information-free rejection. You're not going to hear "This really isn't for us" or any similar brushoffs.

No. You're far more likely to hear something like this:

Mr. Smith: No, no, no, Joan. It's not you. The problem is on this end. Frankly, we're looking for some pretty aggressive terms on our next widget job. And I don't think you can deliver them to us.

Well now. Maybe Mr. Smith is right. Maybe you can't deliver the terms he's after. Then again . . .

However that issue is resolved, you will have smoked the prospect out and found out what was really bothering your contact, and that's the name of the game. When they tell you what's wrong, you can try to correct it.

This is an *extremely* effective technique, but its use is, obviously, limited to one time per prospect. Moreover, you really must stand behind your prospect one hundred percent to be able to pull this approach off. Given those two warnings, you're ready to incorporate this powerful sales tool into your arsenal.

Not infrequently, a prospect will conclude that if you believe in your product that passionately (and, again, you really *must* believe in it passionately for this technique to work), then maybe it's worth looking at a little more closely. Maybe those initial misgivings were a little too conservative. Maybe Mr. Smith will decide it makes sense to consider going with you after all.

CHAPTER EIGHT

SETTING THE APPOINTMENT BY PHONE

With in-person sales appointments costing the average company $250 per visit, it sure pays to make sure field sales reps have a good, solid, qualified appointment to go to—and not a "no thank you" that could have been handled with a thirty-cent phone call.

There are some people who feel that those who set appointments on the telephone but do not close the sale are not, strictly speaking, telemarketers. The argument here is that no real "marketing" takes place during the course of the call, since the person does not intend to close the sale. I think it's a silly debate to get into, since the person on the phone is obviously calling as part of an overall sales effort. For that reason, whether or not they are officially regarded as telemarketers, I'm including a section for this group.

It's worth noting that many of these people are paid on a commission basis once the appointment they set actually yields a paying customer. If getting paid a commission for bringing in a customer doesn't qualify you as a salesperson, I don't know what does! This leads us to the technically intricate—but probably irrelevant—question of whether someone who tries, ultimately, to secure sales by using the phone can be something other than a telemarketer. Who knows. I'll leave the hair-splitting to others and focus on offering sound advice here for getting appointments, no matter what you call yourself or people call you.

There is some common ground between the two types of work. Let's talk for a moment about the similarities between setting an appointment over the phone and closing a sale over the phone.

♦ Each type of call requires you to move through the first three stages of the sales cycle. Of course, you don't have to close if your objective is simply to set an appointment, but some will argue that the act of winning a commitment to make an appointment is similar to the act of closing. Even if your sales close in person rather than over the phone, you will need to negotiate the opening, the information gathering, and the presentation stages properly.

Now and then you will hear some phone salespeople say that the presentation stage can be skipped entirely if the goal is to set the appointment, but I don't buy that. The appointment calls may *abbreviate* the presentation stage somewhat so someone (perhaps the caller) can make a fuller presentation in person, but in my experience these calls never entirely omit it. How can the prospect agree to discuss what has not been presented at all?

♦ Each type of call features objections.

♦ Each type of call is likely to be viewed by the prospect as an interruption of more pressing business, at least at first.

♦ Each type of call requires a script for reference. This "script" must incorporate convincing responses not only for objections, but also for such intermediate queries as "Tell me more" and "What other people/firms have you worked with?" The responses you commit to the script format must, in either environment, sound both convincing and unforced.

◆ Each type of call demands flexibility and the ability to forecast problems ahead of time on the part of the caller. Flexibility is certainly vitally important for the person calling to set the appointment, because the goal there is to leave the call not with something tangible (a sale), but with something abstract (an expression of interest). The caller must therefore allow the prospect to "call the shots" and avoid high-pressure techniques even more assiduously. If you try to strong-arm someone into meeting with your sales rep, you'll probably find that the prospect won't show up!

There are some important differences, as well.

◆ The call to set up the appointment is likely to be somewhat shorter than the call to close over the phone.

◆ The call to set up the appointment is less likely to drift into casual-tone conversation. (Don't misunderstand me here. One of my pet peeves is salespeople—usually novices—who take any opportunity to talk to the prospect for a quarter of an hour about last night's baseball game, the morning traffic, the weather, or any of a hundred other topics that have nothing to do with the real reason behind your call. When you are closing by phone, however, you will find that the development of a one-on-one relationship with the prospect takes on more importance compared with setting appointments by phone, and thus you will often find the feel of the conversation more informal.)

♦ The call to set up the appointment requires much less in the way of an emotional investment from the prospect than the call to close over the phone. After all, deciding to buy something is not something most of us can take lightly these days! Even though time is money, it is considerably easier to get a busy manager to commit to a fifteen-minute visit to *discuss* a new copier system than it is to get him to sign on the bottom line and order one.

Restructuring the Call

Because your call is likely to be shorter than the call made with the intent of closing a sale, you must be more careful about the prospect's attention. In other words, you must do a little more work to make the call as a whole easier for the prospect to understand.

I do a lot of seminars with people who must set appointments by phone for telecommunications companies. Sometimes, when I ask them to tell me what phrasing they use to introduce themselves, I hear something like this:

> Hi, Mr. Smith. My name is John Jones, and I'm calling you from New England Telephone today.

I'm going to argue that, given the fact that you're not going to have too much of the prospect's time *in your best-case scenario*, this opening is not a good idea. Why? Because it leaves the person wondering what went wrong with the mail to make you call to collect on a phone bill! Why set that obstacle in your way? If you are calling from a firm that has an established reputation, you may need to adjust your opening to deal with any preconceptions that may exist in the prospect's mind.

The same problem works in reverse if the opening sounds like this:

> Hi, Mr. Smith. My name is John Jones, and I'm calling you from ABC, Incorporated today.

Can you see where the difficulty is? Can you see that in opening what you know will be a comparatively short call, you have given the prospect absolutely nothing to go on? ABC could be engaged in the manufacture of rocket propellant chemicals for NASA—or it could provide home cleaning services. In a more generous time format, you might be able to support a vague opening like that with a few crisp follow-up senctences. Not here, though.

When you are dealing with the inherent time restraints of appointment-based calling, give your firm a very brief "commercial" right up front. Your call's opening might sound something like either of these examples:

> *You:* Good morning, Mr. Smith. This is John Jones calling from ABC, Incorporated. I'm not sure if you're familiar with us, but we're the largest manufacturers of widgets in the greater Wichita area. How are you today?

> *You:* Good morning, Mr. Smith. This is John Jones calling from Cellular Phones, Unlimited. How are you today?

You're now going to continue through an abbreviated version of the pitch designed for closing the sale over the phone. Don't blink; you might miss the stages as they pass! (Note that the pauses for prospect "assent" to move through the stages are less important in this type of call.)

You: The reason I'm calling you today, Mr. Smith, is to introduce you to our widget upgrade service. Do you presently have a widget in your home, Mr. Smith?

Mr. Smith: Yes, I do.

You: Well, I think you'll probably be interested, sir, because we've been able to save homeowners in your area an average of fifteen percent in the first month alone. That can total thousands of dollars—and these days, that kind of money is worth trying to save! What we're doing today is giving area homeowners the chance to take a look at our program in a little more detail. I'd like to stop by to tell you about some of the things we've been doing with other people in the Middleton area to save them money. Would this Saturday at two be a good time?

If you examine the above closely, you'll find a single question (the abbreviated information-gathering stage), a short description of the product or service (the presentation), and an assumptive request for a meeting time (this parallels the assumptive close).

Here's a common roadblock faced by many people who must set appointments by phone—and a way around it:

Mr. Smith: I can't set an appointment. I'm just too busy.

You: Well, Mr. Jones, I don't know what your schedule looks like—but do you think we can get together on [date approximately thirty days from now]?

Such an approach will usually separate the legitimately harried from those who simply use "scheduling conflicts" as an all-purpose excuse to end the conversation. (How many of us are "tied up" for every possible slot over the next thirty days?)

This, of course, brings us back to objections. Remember the "Can-I-ask-a-question" technique:

> *You:* What we're doing today is giving area home-owners the chance to take a look at our program in a little more detail. I'd like to stop by to tell you about some of the things we've been . . .

> *Mr. Smith:* Let me stop you right there. I don't think that will be necessary. I'm very happy with what I have right now.

> *You:* Well, Mr. Smith, can I ask you one question?

> *Mr. Smith:* Sure.

> *You:* Just out of curiosity, how are you presently meeting your widget needs?

> *Mr. Smith:* [Any answer.]

Again, you are going to tend to get a "yes" to your request because the prospect will often want to appear reasonable in dealing with you after issuing what could be perceived as a negative. ("I'm really very happy with what I have right now.") If and when you confront the negative again, you can respond with the All-Purpose Turnaround:

> *Mr. Smith:* I hate to cut you short, Joan, but I really am happy with my present service.

> *You:* Mr. Smith, I have to tell you something. That is exactly how most of my current customers reacted to the program before I had the chance to show them how we could cut their widget bills by fifteen percent. I'd like to do the same for

you. Do you think we could talk about it this
Friday at three?

"You Want Me to Say What?"

The short, sweet approach I've just outlined scares a lot
of salespeople—at first. They say things like, "Do I really
have to *say* that to him?"

Well, no. There are certainly a lot of other things you
can say. But I will tell you here and now that not one of
them will work as well in setting up appointments as
what I'm advocating.

My way is direct, honest, and to the point. It tells the
prospect what's happening, proposes a way to help solve a
problem, and asks for the date. You don't *have* to use it, of
course, but you really should . . . because it works. Once you
do give it a try, I have a feeling you'll be pleasantly surprised enough to want to stick with it.

If You Are Setting Appointments for Yourself by Calling Prospects Who Have Responded to a "Cold" Mass Mailing . . .

Consider the following approach.

> *You:* Mr. Smith, the reason I'm calling is that you re-
> turned the reply card included with our recent
> mailing. And I have to tell you, sir, a lot of peo-
> ple have been sending that card in! The re-
> sponse has certainly been an overwhelming
> positive for us. I wanted to get in touch with
> you today to let you know that I'll be visiting
> some of the homeowners in your area next
> week. I'm scheduling my time right now, and
> I'll be passing through your neighborhood next
> Thursday evening at about six o'clock. I wanted
> to know if I could stop by then.

That's the entire call. When I give this outline to the salespeople in my seminars, they're often flabbergasted. What about the probing questions? What about the explanations, the alternatives, the comparisons with the competition?

In this case, you can elminate all those concerns from your call. Remember, the prospect has *already qualfied himself* by contacting you, and may even be expecting the call. If only all our sales calls could operate under such circumstances!

You can fill in all the blanks during the in-person visit. The technique I've outlined may seem a little too straightforward at first, but I believe you will be quite happy with the results if you give it an honest try.

Don't play around with the dates by blizzarding the prospect with choices: "Would you prefer to meet on the evening of Monday the third or Wednesday the fifth?" Instead, select a single date when you will be in the area to visit other prospects. Propose that date and see what happens.

If You Are Calling "Cold" Prospects to Set Appointments for Someone Else . . .

Let's say your call is the kind that sounds like this:

> *You:* Mr. Smith, I'll tell you what I'd love to do. I work with another salesperson, Michael Smith, who's going to be in the Pittsburgh area next week to visit Pittsburgh Concrete Products. I think it would be a great idea for him to stop in and see you on Friday. Would two o'clock be good?

One thing's certain. Those who phone to set up appointments for others have a number of unique challenges to address.

After all, they run the risk of being somewhat removed from the sales process. If you do this kind of work you should, ideally, view the salesperson who closes the sale as your teammate—but it is easy to fall short of the ideal. You're not the person actually closing the sale; it may be a little easier for you to become cavalier about qualifying the prospect, especially considering that you will be calling for extended periods of time without interruption. You should bear this built-in handicap in mind as you make your calls. You may need to review the earlier chapter on the stages of the sale for an occasional refresher on the importance of conducting the information gathering stage properly.

The second hurdle people in this type of sales position face is more immediate: Prospects often ask them questions they can't answer. This is easy enough to remedy if you work in an open environment where you can get the help you need to find the correct answer, but, unfortunately, some sales managers view responding to these queries as relatively unimportant. If your sales manager views your job as essentially clerical or routine in nature, and if it is therefore difficult or impossible for you to get the information you need to resolve legitimate customer inquiries, you may well be working for the wrong company. Unresponsive sales managers who urge appointment-setting personnel to "just focus on the numbers" rather than build relationships with clients are probably expecting you to burn out sooner or later and leave the position. In such a case, it will probably be better for you to secure employment elsewhere and make your departure date sooner rather than later.

Helpful Hints

Here are some general suggestions that will help you to be more effective in your efforts to set sales appointments.

1. Compose and work with your script. My experience has been that many salespeople who set sales appointments want to "wing it" because they feel doing so sounds more spontaneous to the prospect. There is a virtue in making your pitch sound fresh, but not if it comes at the expense of your own preparation. As you have no doubt gathered by now, I am an enthusiastic proponent of abandoning the automaton school of phone sales. Still, that doesn't mean you can wander into the call unprepared. Script your work and work your script.

2. Set specific goals. Try to reach decision-makers fifty percent of the time. Try to schedule appointments with one out of three decision-makers. Try to maintain a fifty-percent closing ratio for all appointments you schedule. (Obviously, these numbers will vary slightly from industry to industry, but they nevertheless represent good target levels in the vast majority of cases.)

3. If you are also the person making the in-person visits, be sure to allot a certain amount of time every day for calls. Doing so will help you keep those sales coming "through the pipeline." Your daily appointment with yourself to make the calls leads to the two or three daily appointments you will need to be successful.

4. Mentally review your calls after you've made them. Where could you have reacted more effectively to a prospect's concern or problem? Was there a point at which you tried to move the prospect along too soon? Do you find yourself hemming and hawing when it comes time to schedule the visit? Keep a watchful eye out for signs of any of these problems, and follow

the advice from earlier sections of this book in overcoming them.

5. If your job is to set appointments for someone else, schedule a time to meet with the salesperson who will be going on the appointments you schedule. Do a roleplaying exercise together in which that sales rep tries to sell you the product. Maintain regular contact with this salesperson so you can keep each other abreast of new developments.

6. If you are setting appointments for someone else, pay particularly close attention to the number of appointments you schedule and the quality of the appointments you schedule. Hitting or exceeding the fifty-percent closing target on, say, four appointments enough probably means you are overqualifying and should review your technique. You are probably losing your company customers by setting your appointment standards too high. On the other hand, missing the fifty-percent mark by a wide margin but posting many, many appointments is probably an indication that your qualifying could use some tightening.

7. If you are setting appointments for another person, don't talk about "my representative." Use the salesperson's name: "Frank McCartin is our representative in your area."

8. Avoid phrases like, "Jane Fox will be in your area this Tuesday." That implies that your company has so little to do that it can pay people to hang around on streetcorners. Instead, highlight success and professional competence by saying something like "Our representative Jane Fox

will be in the West Side area this week to meet with the people over at ABC Manufacturing, and I'd love to set up an appoint with you, too. How is Tuesday at two?"

For a more detailed discussion of the best ways to handle the appointment call, you might want to take a look at a copy of my earlier book *Cold Calling Techniques (That Really Work!).*

CHAPTER NINE

THE NUMBERS

Even if you're not big on math, you'll want to go over this chapter with a fine-toothed comb. For my part, I'm terrible with figures—but I wouldn't part with the principles in this part of the book on a bet.

Let me begin with a promise: This part of the system is simple. I've kept it simple because I want it to be easy for you to incorporate what follows into your routine—permanently. If you do so, you will be taking a giant step toward increasing your telemarketing income potential in both the short and long term.

If you follow the advice of only one chapter in this book, you should make it this one. Do exactly what is outlined below and you are sure to see dramatic positive results in your telemarketing work in only a week or two.

◆　　◆　　◆

Get a standard notepad and keep a log of your calls. Do this in the following way:

1. Make four columns with the following head-
   ings: Dials, Completed Calls, Presentations, Successes.

2. Every time you dial the phone and hear anything other than your own dial tone, give yourself a tic mark in the Dials column. That means
   you give yourself a tic mark for reaching a
   wrong number, a message that tells you the
   number you want has been disconnected, or for
   actually reaching the number you want.

3. Every time you reach a decision-maker—
   someone who, on his or her own authority,
   could see that you attain the objective of your
   call—give yourself a tic mark in the Completed Calls column.

4. Every time you are able to hold a legitimate,
   open-minded discussion with that decision-
   maker about the possibility of using your product or service, give yourself a tic mark in the
   Presentations column.

5. Every time your call ends successfully, give
   yourself a tic mark under the Successes column.
   That means you get a tic mark for setting an appointment if the goal of your call is to set an appointment, but not if the goal of your call is to
   make a sale. (See the earlier chapter on types of
   sales calls if you have any confusion at all about
   the objective of your call.)

After you've posted a day's worth of tic marks, total
everything up. File these daily numbers and continue the
process for at least two weeks.

The ratio of these combined totals will help you understand how well you're doing and will help you focus on

where you need improvement. You'll be able to see, for instance, that it takes you ninety dials to yield fifty completed calls, fifteen presentations, and five successes. In addition, you'll be able to chart daily variations from your standard patterns.

Now, let's suppose you define a "success" as closing a sale, and let's further assume that your sales manager sits you down and tells you that you "need to improve this week." Sales managers are famous for saying utterly vapid things like that. Fine, you may think to yourself. I'm supposed to improve my numbers. But *how*?

Here's how. Let's say you want seven sales per day instead of five. What do you have to do to make those two extra sales? Well, using the numbers we gave above, we can see that each sale really breaks down to eighteen dials. Two times eighteen is thirty-six, so the question is whether or not you can up your daily dialing total to 126. The answer is probably yes! Now you have a specific step you can take to achieve the goal you've identified. You're going to concentrate on hitting those thirty-six extra dials—and not on "giving it everything you've got," "really reaching out to get new customers," "making that last call of the day," or any other similarly vague objectives. (Of course, if you wanted to focus on other areas than your dialing totals, we could have defined the sale in terms of how many completed calls or presentations you made.)

This system is a must for anyone doing any kind of selling by phone—not only because it allows you to analyze your own progress in the way we've just seen, but also because it proves once and for all that *every step you take along the way is essential to your success*! You may not have thought of reaching disconnected numbers or talking to prospects who don't want your product as keys to closing sales, but I think you can see now that they really are. After all, every dial works in your favor. The bigger your net, the more fish you will catch. Some are going to slip away, but once you accept that as part of the overall process, you can view your efforts in the proper perspective.

In my seminars, I often suggest counting the rejections and letting the sales take care of themselves. This approach is generally greeted by sales managers with a wild-eyed panic usually seen only in stock traders and nervous politicians. "What do you mean, you want them to focus on the rejects? What will that do to their outlook? How do you know it won't steer my salespeople toward burnout?" Even with all the heat I've taken from sales managers on this point, I've stuck by the suggestion—because it works. It reduces the pressure rather than increasing it. When you know the rejections are going to come, you don't take them personally! You can relax and get them out of the way! You don't freeze up as much! One company I did a program for let me offer one of their skeptical sales reps a cash "commission" for every rejection she received, as long as she hit a certain level. She hit it—and posted her personal best in *real* commissions at the same time!

You may or may not decide to focus on the rejections in this way, but I would argue that you should at the very least be able to *determine* your rejection rate if you want to. Once you have identified your personal calling figures—and I would suggest you take the figures from at least two weeks to look at— you can set your own goals, determine the best ways to achieve them, and, last but not least, keep that pesky sales manager happy. For a while, anyway.

Helpful Hints

The following are some good general guidelines you should follow in monitoring your sales figures.

1. Always track your numbers. Period. Do not do any phone work for any period of time without monitoring your call totals in a notebook.

2. Set specific goals. Try to reach decision-makers fifty percent of the time. Try to schedule appointments with one out of three decision-makers. Try to maintain a fifty-percent closing ratio for all appointments you schedule. (Obviously, these numbers will vary slightly from industry to industry, but they nevertheless represent good target levels in the vast majority of cases.)

PART III

FOR THE LONG HAUL

CHAPTER TEN

THREE TOOLS FOR SUCCESS

In this chapter we will take a look at three vitally important tools for success—tools that are almost universally ignored by telemarketers.

It's hard to say exactly why telemarketers don't take advantage of these sales success tools. My guess is that a good percentage of them feel as though they aren't "real" salespeople, and that they consider the measures below to be the exclusive domain of those who close sales in person. As I noted earlier in the book, you must consider your telemarketing job your "real" job if you hope to develop a professional image and boost your sales performance.

With that in mind, review the following sales tools and try to find ways you can work them into your routine. It is, after all, your career—and your career is worth a little extra effort.

Tool Number One: The Personal Contact Network

That person you were just introduced to at the party is more than a new acquaintance. He's a potential prospect—and/or someone who can introduce you to another potential prospect.

Don't be shy. Tell everyone what you do—every chance you get. And do it proudly. Whether you've been selling for a week, or a month, or a year, or every day of your life, you should always be ready to talk about what you do for a living to anyone and everyone who'll listen. Word of mouth is one of the most cost-effective ways to solicit leads; the people you talk to may well know others who could use your product or service.

For some strange reason, telemarketers don't want to do this. They go to a social event, they meet people, they talk, and when one of the most common questions of all—"What do you do for a living?"—comes up, what does the salesperson say? Or, more accurately, whisper? Out comes this barely audible confession: "I, ah . . . I sell widgets . . .", or, "I'm involved in some marketing-related projects, just now, that is . . .", or "Me? Oh, I, well, I work in this bank."

Why don't you hear the person booming out proudly, "I sell financial services for XYZ Bank!"? Try it. Take the initiative. Tell people what you do without waiting for them to ask.

This is a secret most successful people swear by. Let the word get out about how well you do your job and how great your product is. Before too long, you'll hear from someone inquiring about your product or service before too long.

Let me give you a real-life example of what I'm talking about. You're probably familiar with the name Joe Girard—he's the guy who holds the honor of having sold three times more Chevrolets than any other person on earth. Joe made a single, breathtaking discovery—and that discovery is what made it possible for him to become a true sales superstar. He found that 100% of the people he came in contact with would eventually either need a car, or be able to introduce him to someone who did. That principle is easy enough to extend to your situation.

If Mr. Jones, whom you meet at a party, doesn't use widgets in his operation, but knows all sorts of people who do, there's no law against tactfully passing on your business card. And there's no law against asking him, tactfully and professionally, if he knows of anyone who might benefit from your product. If he supplies you with a couple of names and gives you permission to mention the fact that he suggested you call, you know what you've got? The kind of telemarketing leads that dreams are made of!

Tool Number Two: Your Initiative

Perhaps to a greater extent than any other professional occupation, sales demands a great deal in terms of individual initiative and the ability to motivate oneself.

Now, when most people hear the word "motivate," their eyes glaze over a little bit as they prepare for a lecture about how important it is to get in to the office on time in the morning. That's not what I'm talking about. When I talk about motivation, I mean taking on the responsibility to affect your environment in such a way that your sales efforts will be more profitable for you. Period.

The beauty of sales in general and telemarketing in particular lies in your ability to control your own destiny. Nobody else is calling up your clients, presenting your product, taking down your orders. And the degree to which you allow outside forces to determine your rate of success is, in my view, the degree to which your initiative has failed you.

Recently, as one of my seminars was drawing to a close, I was talking to a salesperson about his approach to his job. It was in the middle of the summer. "It's a tough month to sell, August," he told me. "Once we head into the fall, I'll do all right."

"It's true," I said. "August, everyone's on vacation. Can't sell during August, can you? You know what, though, a lot of the decision-makers save up their vacation time and go in September. Who knows where they go, but it seems like they sure aren't in the office. So you can't sell in September. Then there's October. God, I hate October, don't you? Everybody's mind is filled with football and the World Series. You really can't get anything accomplished in October. Then there's November. Half the offices quit early for Thanksgiving; you've got the longest long weekend of them all right there. November— write it off. Then—watch out— HAPPY HOLIDAYS! They're all out shopping, drives me nuts, but you sure can't get any sales in December. January, it's off to Aruba or Club Med or wherever they find to go, so you can't get any selling done in January. February, the darned *month* is short on days, so what do they do? Stuff it with three-day weekends, that's what! March, the weather's so foul, who wants to go on appointments. When April comes around, nobody wants to talk business—they all want to take advantage of the nice weather they haven't seen for months. Same thing for May. June is okay, you can get in the door, but you'll always hear, 'Wait till after the quarter's over, we'll have a better idea then.' I don't like June too much, to tell you the truth.

"July's all right. What a way to make a living, though: one month out of the year!" He agreed with me—and his career is over!

Sending yourself negative messages like, "August is a tough month to sell" takes events out of your hands. Sending yourself positive messages like "Today is a great day to sell!" puts you right back where you belong: in control. Tough month or no tough month, August or no August, there you are with a job to do. Whose show is this, anyway? Yours? Or August's?

Tool Number Three: Your Filing System

Don't "wing it." Keep immaculately organized files. And keep an eye open for new filing systems that will help you become even more efficient.

You might consider using a prospecting board. Here's how it works: Once you've called a prospect, rate him or her by category on a bulletin board. The categories reflect the likelihood, in your estimation, of closing the sale.

Let's look at my sales environment to give you an idea of how this might work. I handle sales training programs. If I speak to a manager at a bank who tells me that the company is thinking of hiring a sales trainer, but can't really give it serious consideration until a major project is completed six weeks from now, I'll put that in my "B" category. I reserve that category for prospects I feel have a fifty-fifty chance of closing. If, on the other hand, I visit a shipping company vice-president who explains that he needs to line up a guest speaker for the firm's yearly sales meeting, and then asks how long it would take to forward my rates for a three-day seminar, I'm going to feel that the likelihood of closing is pretty good. That's an "A" prospect, and from experience I've learned that I'll close that sale something like nine times out of ten. (There's also the "C" category: the "hmm-sounds-interesting-we'll-get-back-to-you" group. I can usually close about 30% of these prospects.)

After talking to twenty people, my prospecting board may look something like this:

DATE	A	B	C
Monday	✔	✔✔	✔✔✔
	✔	✔✔✔	✔✔✔
	✔	✔	✔✔✔
			✔✔✔

A prospect board like this tells me that my leads are pretty good. I've got three "A" clients I should definitely close. I've got six in that "B" category, and finally, I've got that list of twelve "C" prospects I'm developing. The key word here is "developing." I'm constantly working with this board in order to adjust the prospects—in other words, turn the "C" contacts into "A" contacts.

I should offer you one word of warning—that "C" category is much more important than it appears at first glance. In many cases, my "C" group will supply prospects that upgrade to my "B" group, which in turn supplies some candidates for my "A" group.

It's always going to be tempting to hammer away at the "A" prospects and close the sales. And I may not need encouragement when it comes to plugging away at the "B" group. But keeping a good batch of "C" candidates on the board means I will always have something to upgrade, something to help me keep the system moving.

Another popular filing tool is the old shoe-box method, which allows you to store index cards that represent your prospects according to your own sort system. Personally, I prefer a notebook. A shoebox system doesn't allow you to put in photocopies of the correspondence you've had with the client, or any of the notes you may make during your work. What's worse, index cards don't allow you enough space to record much information.

What actually goes into the files on individual contacts you hope to turn into customers? That will depend on your own preferences. For my part, I'm not in favor of going overboard on researching each prospect I see. I know a lot of salespeople feel that they really have to know all the details on a given prospect in order to close the sale. And, to a certain extent, that may be true: If you're selling a component for use in a large, expensive computer system, you really do need to know whether or not the company has that system. But, beyond that basic information, I can tell you that it's simply not true that a sale depends on heroic amounts of research time.

Try to keep in mind that the professional telemarketer is really more of a conduit than a consultant. What I mean by that is, you're the medium through which the prospect can have his or her technical concerns addressed—you're not responsible for possessing all the knowledge about the prospect necessary to address those concerns. It's more important to have a good, broad sense of the overriding demographics of your target group than it is to know what any one individual prospect has for breakfast on Thursday mornings. Use your files as a tool—not as an end unto themselves.

CHAPTER ELEVEN

PRODUCT MALLEABILITY

In this chapter, we'll be looking at one of the most important ways you can set yourself apart from amateurish "automaton" telemarketers: highlighting product malleability.

What is product malleability? It's knowing how to make your product or service fit somewhere else. To do this, you must know what you sell very well—and you must develop the capacity to think creatively about consumer needs. By meeting these two demands, you will be setting yourself apart from the vast majority of the robots out there armed with calling lists.

Technically, "malleability" means flexibility, the capacity to adapt well to new situations and requirements. You may be familiar with the term as it refers to metals. For example, dentists use gold and silver for fillings because those metals are easy to manipulate and can provide a secure fit over and within a cavity. Can your product or service fill a variety of different "holes" easily?

Consider the paper clip. Most of us think of it as a simple device used to fasten a number of sheets of paper together. But how many *different* uses can you come up with? Stop and think for a moment. Pull out a piece of paper and write down all the possible additional uses one might find for the standard metal paper clip. Close the book now, then come back and compare your answers to the ones that follow.

◆　◆　◆

A paper clip can be a . . .

◆ Decorative element (chains, miniature sculptures, mobiles)

◆ Cleaning utensil for small nooks and crannies of office equipment

◆ Makeshift keyring

◆ Eyeglass repair component

◆ Improvised cotter pin

◆ Part of a two-clip "tweezer" used to extract a disk that won't eject from a computer drive

◆ Stabilizing component for a wobbly paper airplane

◆ Part of a makeshift compass

◆ Means of picking a lock

◆ Emergency writing implement (use end to carve letters into hard surface)

◆ Fingernail cleaner

◆ Unit of measure (when straightened)

◆ Projectile with offensive capability (with rubber band)

◆　◆　◆

These are just a few of the possible additional uses for a simple metal paper clip. You may have came up with a few that didn't appear on the list. Wonderful! If you kept at it, you could probably come up with a hundred different uses for that paper clip.

Well, now. Are there a hundred different uses for your product or service—uses that you may never have considered before, but that a prospect might find appealing? Take the time to brainstorm. Write your ideas down, even the outlandish ones. After all, you don't *need* a hundred new applications to stand out from the crowd. You need one. Let your imagination run wild. You can edit out the weaker uses later.

If you look around you, you'll see firms applying this concept to all kinds of products and services. Once upon a time, the only people who had beepers were white-collar business professionals. Now expectant fathers of many economic levels use them to be able to have the soonest possible word on when labor pains begin. People used to think of baking soda as something you cooked with, period. Now the Arm and Hammer people have convinced consumers of the benefits of buying two boxes: one for the cupboard, and one to keep the refrigerator smelling fresh and clean. I know a couple of people who brush their teeth with the stuff!

If you manage Stage Two correctly, you will be in a great position to suggest other uses for your product or service. What's more, once you've established one or more areas of product malleability, you will have found a way to turn around some of your pre-Stage Two objections. Finally, you may be able to enhance satisfaction among your present customers. These are not the hallmarks of an amateur!

CHAPTER TWELVE

THE STORY

Good salespeople are good communicators. Good communicators are people who tell good stories.

I don't mean to suggest that you should pass along the jokes or anecdotes you might hear at a party, and I'm certainly not suggesting you fabricate anything. These approaches will not lead to sales success. I *am* suggesting that you familiarize yourself with good, solid examples of how your product or service can help other people just like your prospect.

The kinds of stories I'm suggesting have already been touched on during our earlier discussions of the All-Purpose Turnaround. There, however, the references to satisfied customers you made were brief—because they had to be. You had only a few seconds to overcome an initial objection, so you made a one- or two-sentence reference to a success story that followed skepticism very similar to the prospect's current skepticism.

In other settings, you will be able to expand on these success stories. You will be able to use them at your own discretion during the sales cycle to build the prospect's confidence, focus attention on product or service strengths, and customize your presentation in such a way that the prospect receives messages targeted directly to the resolution of his or her problems.

The key word here is "customized." You want to find as many direct parallels with the environment your prospect faces as possible. The more your prospect feels that the success story is "just like me," the more likely you're going to be to close the sale when the moment of truth arrives.

Try to determine exactly what your prospect's objective with regard to your product or service is. Perhaps that objective is to increase sales. Perhaps it's·to streamline operations and work more efficiently. Perhaps it's to resolve a pressing problem that's come up without warning and is keeping him or her from focusing on more important issues. Whatever the objective, supply, if you can, a true story from your firm's past history that has the following features:

◆ A person in a predicament similar to the prospect's. (*Not* "The ABC Company." Your story should concern a person by the name of Frank Smith who happens to work at ABC. Organizations are cold and remote; people with real problems live in the same world you and I do.)

◆ The sense that "all was lost." (Get the idea across that the person you eventually helped was really in deep trouble and had no idea where to turn.)

◆ The successful resolution of the problem by your firm— *after* a minimal struggle or a temporary setback you managed to overcome. (It's important to make your record look believable. A dose of real-world adversity—deftly handled by your organization, of course—will make it clear that you're not selling something too good to be true.)

Here are some examples of the kinds of stories you might be on the lookout for. Remember, you must adapt real, honest-to-goodness success stories involving your product or service. Making things up out of whole cloth will inevitably come back to haunt you, as will trying to pound a story into shape to make it suit a prospect in another customer group.

> *YOU:* You know, the situation you're looking at now reminds me a little of the one that Joyce Reynolds over at Webster Engineering was facing. She had underestimated her monthly widget use by forty percent. I mean, she was way off the mark, and the people in Accounting were getting ready to launch a major revolt. Everything looked terrible for her—she was afraid she wasn't going to be able to come close to meeting her yearly numbers. When she called us, she was about ready to throw in the towel. But what she found was that by transferring over to our Model Nine widgets, she'd end up boosting productivity significantly even though the up-front costs were a little higher than what she was using. She ended up going over budget by only two percent—as opposed to the twenty-five or thirty percent she was worried about.

> *YOU:* I have to tell you, Mr. Smith, there's a man by the name of Michael Powers over at Berkley Technical Products who had a problem very similar to yours. The sales staff at BTP just wasn't hitting the numbers people had hoped for, and that was really taking its toll. Not only were they losing ground to the competition in some very important markets, but they found that their salespeople were so unhappy that the turnover rate at Berkley was about twice the industry average. When I first talked to Mike, he was extremely worried about his department. I told him about our prospecting program and

about the successes we had been having with some of the other companies in his field. He was reluctant at first, but I think he was concerned enough about the performance of his people that he knew he had to make a change somewhere. He went with us, and I'm happy to pass along that their sales over six months increased thirty percent after our two-week program. Their turnover rates this year look a lot better, too.

YOU: You know, Mr. Smith, what you're describing to me really rings a bell. We worked with a firm in Orlando, Florida called First Word Publishing. They were having real problems hitting their deadlines; the editor there, a woman by the name of Dawn Myers, had simply overloaded her production department. I talked to Dawn about some of the things we could offer her; her initial reaction was that a book development service such as ours would be too expensive. But she agreed to work with us on a trial basis because she was under such a severe time crunch. That worked out very well. In fact, we've now brought in seven books for Dawn on time and on or under budget. My feeling is that we're a very important part of the planning at First Word now. I have a job I'm working on with them right now.

YOU: Mr. Smith, let me give you an example of what we've been able to do for some of the companies in your area. There's a firm here in Fairwell County known as Magnasource; the office manager is a very pleasant gentleman, David Riley, and he had a huge problem with his phone system. Customers were being disconnected; messages weren't getting through; calls were being misrouted. It was a mess. I told David we could turn things around for him in less than three days. He was skeptical, but he was also tired of apologizing to customers who'd been cut off. Sure enough, we had a system that fit his budget, and three days later he was up and running with a message-forwarding system that improved Magnasource's image to phone customers dramatically.

YOU: Mr. Smith, I'd like to tell you about an event we put together for United Teleconference. They were throwing a huge party to mark their twenty-fifth anniversary, and they needed a caterer who could provide them with nothing but the best. My contact there was a man named Martin Johnson, and he was extremely concerned about quality—because he had a very bad experience with another caterer at a previous company event. The serving people had arrived late, the food was cold, even the silverware was dirty. I gave Mr. Johnson a detailed list of everything we would be providing for his event, he decided to give us a chance, and everything came off perfectly.

Of course, it is worth noting once again that you should clear any such use of actual names ahead of time with the principals of your story. This is generally no problem; most people are flattered by the attention!

CHAPTER THIRTEEN

KEEPING IT FRESH

Most telemarketers make hundreds of calls every week. They say the same thing, or slight variations on it, over and over again. They re-fashion their material into a form that suits the particular occasion, but they wonder, at times, about their ability to keep the message lively and upbeat. There is a constant challenge to keep the repetitive nature of phone sales work from detracting from the quality of each individual call. How do you do it?

The best way is simply to keep in mind that each contact you deal with really is a brand new person who is incapable of having the same sense of familiarity about your presentation you do *because he or she has never heard it before.* Because we hear the message so many times, we tend to lose sight of the prospect's position. If we can keep from becoming jaded, hurried, or overpresumptious, each new contact really does represent a new, uncharted frontier. Even if we've made the pitch a thousand times before, each call is a brand new opportunity. Your door is open by default—not closed.

Paradoxically enough, you must sometimes worry less about keeping things fresh for you, and more about keeping things relevant and comprehensible for the prospect. Have you ever found yourself throwing new elements into your presentation because you were afraid the old stuff would seem boring? If you knew the old approaches (to, say, a familiar objection) were effective, the odds are that you were making a serious mistake. After all, it's not whether or not *you* get bored that counts, but the prospect's assessment of your message. That prospect has never heard you before, remember?

In his excellent book *High Impact Telephone Networking for Job Hunters,* Howard Armstrong offers a telling analogy that touches on just this issue. He relates how he went to see a production of a hit Broadway show that had been playing for some months, and found himself wondering what it was that kept the cast members so well focused. After all, here was a group of people who had been saying the same lines in the same order and in the same theater literally hundreds of nights running. Yet their performances seemed fresh, competent, and enthusiastic. He as an audience member certainly couldn't have asked for anything more. How did they pull it off?

Then the answer hit him. As the actors look out across the footlights, they sense not just another crowd—but a group of real live individuals. They each make eye contact with a particular audience member, someone who *hasn't* seen the show four hundred times. Well, you, too, have to look out across the footlights and project to the new person you meet on each call. That "audience member" is taking you in for the first time!

Forget what's gone before. All you have to work with is this moment, the one right in front of you, right now, if you want to impress that "producer." But that's plenty.

PART IV

SOME FINAL THOUGHTS

CHAPTER FOURTEEN

THE MOST COMMON QUESTIONS

In this chapter, we'll focus on the answers to some of the most popular questions salespeople pose during my seminars with them.

"How should I deal with the secretary?"

Too many telemarketers treat the secretary as a natural enemy. This is a mistake.

The professional telemarketer will recognize that the secretary, too, has a role to play in the business world. Strive to get this "gatekeeper" to work with you.

Ask yourself: What is the secretary's main function, the standard by which his or her day is judged? Clearly, it is to maximize the boss's productivity and ability to achieve goals. There's nothing subversive in that. As a potential vendor to the company, you probably want the boss's efficiency to be pretty high yourself, because you want this customer to succeed and stick around for a while. So there's some common ground.

Adjust your attitude. Keep in mind that you are dealing with a person who can help you . . . *if* you show clearly that you are acting in accordance with his or her goals and responsibilities. Consider approaching the secretary with a message that highlights the benefits to the buyer and mentions the (modest!) amount of time you will require for your phone call. Ask the secretary to help you arrange that call. Make sure he or she is aware of the benefit the boss is likely to reap by working with you.

> *You:* Ms. Ryan, may I ask for your help in arranging a time to reach Mr. Smith sometime during the next two weeks? This is regarding a structured approach to the widget problem; it's been used by many firms in your industry to increase earnings.

This direct, honest tone can be especially effective with secretaries who have grown used to treating all telemarketers as enemies. (That may well be the majority of all secretaries these days.)

The secretary may ask for more information. Be polite and continue to give a *general* outline of what you propose. Don't fall into the trap of treating the secretary as the prospect. The goal should be to schedule a time to speak with the boss—not to win the secretary's interest.

If you continue to have problems getting through, consider calling before or after the secretary's working hours. You will often be able to reach the boss directly.

"Are there certain 'power words' I should try to weave into my presentation?"
　　　Yes. Consider the entries on the following list.
　　　Bargain
　　　Clean
　　　Efficient
　　　Elegance
　　　Essential

Genuine
Growth
Guaranteed
Health
High-growth
Independent
Low-cost
Modern
Necessary
Popular
Progress Proven
Quality
Recommended
Reputation
Rugged
Scientific
Stylish
Successful
Tested
Thinking
Time-saving
Up-to-date
Value

"How do I reach the prospects who never seem to be in?"

Knowing when to call—or, perhaps more accurately, when *not* to call—your prospect is an important part of your job.

You wouldn't call someone who owns a small restaurant at twelve noon, sharp—even if you knew the person would be there at that time. Calling then would be pointless, because your contact would almost certainly be involved in handling the lunch rush. Whatever goodwill your call might engender at a non-rush time would be quickly overshadowed by the events of the moment.

Trying to call a gift or book retailer for *any* reason at *any* time of day between the fifteenth and twenty-fourth of December is similarly pointless. The Christmas shopping season will be in full swing, and the only result of your call will be to further exhaust and harry the person trying to keep track of it all.

Following is a list of the best suggested times to reach various categories of prospects by phone.

Accountants: Standard business hours *except* between January 15th and April 15th.

Bankers: Before ten in the morning and after three in the afternoon, Monday through Friday.

Clergy: Between Tuesday and Friday.

Dentists: Between nine and eleven in the morning, Monday through Friday.

Doctors: Before nine-thirty in the morning or after one-thirty in the afternoon, Monday through Friday.

Engineers: Between one and five in the afternoon, Monday through Friday.

Executives: Before nine in the morning, during the lunch hour, and after one-thirty in the afternoon, Monday through Friday.

Farmers: Between noon and one in the afternoon.

General Contractors: Before nine in the morning, during the lunch hour, and after five in the afternoon, Monday through Friday.

Grocers: Between one and three in the afternoon.

Heads of
businesses: Before nine in the morning, during the lunch hour, and after five in the afternoon, Monday through Friday.

Homemakers: Between ten and eleven-thirty in the morning, and between two and four o'clock in the afternoon.

Lawyers: Between eleven in the morning and two in the afternoon, and betwen four and five in the afternoon.

Nurses: During the half-hour before or after scheduled duty hours; these will vary from person to person. (You might want to call the hospital to get more details on the shift schedules.)

Pharmacists: Between one and three in the afternoon.

Teachers: Between two in the afternoon and six in the evening, Monday through Friday.

You'll get the best information on when to try to reach your prospects—and when not to—by developing a knowledge base about your own business area. Track your calls—are a substatial number of the calls you make at a certain time of day getting nowhere because your contacts are otherwise occupied? Are calls you make at "nonstandard" times—after five in the afternoon or before nine in the morning—yielding better-than-average results?

Once you've determined your "prime time," you will be able to manage your time much more effectively. Many people cost themselves sizable commissions because their personal rhythms dictate that they do paperwork at a time when they would be best advised trying to reach customers. Don't be one of them! Use your time wisely.

"What are the most common telemarketing mistakes?"

In my experience, the most common errors among telemarketers are the items listed below.

1. Failure to vary tonal delivery; related voice tone problems.

2. Speaking too quickly or too slowly.

3. Calling without good goal orientation.

4. Failing to qualify properly; making the presentation to the wrong person.

5. Offering the prospect too much information.

6. Not giving the prospect a reason to continue listening.

7. Not establishing what the prospect does and how he or she does it.

8. Making unwarranted assumptions about the prospect's past history.

9. Assuming that the prospect knows more about the product or service than he or she actually does.

10. Forgetting the importance of maintaining a relaxed, conversational tone.

CHAPTER FIFTEEN

THE ROAD FROM HERE

Finally—you're ready to put this system to work.

I'll leave you with a parting thought about a very simple idea: commitment. The ideas in this book will work for you to the degree that you make a personal commitment to implementing them. Merely knowing about the techniques will gain you nothing.

I've mentioned in my other books that most experts agree that it takes twenty-one days to adopt a good habit or rid oneself of a bad one. I'm going to suggest you use that approach here. Now that you've completed this book, give the ideas contained within it a fair try for twenty-one consecutive work days. My bet is that you'll be very pleased with the results you see. We've talked a lot about professionalism in this book; I will leave you with a thought from one of my favorite writers, Robert Louis Stevenson, that seems to me to do justice to the topic, and to offer a valuable definition of professionalism. Stevenson wrote, "If a man love the labour of any trade apart from any question of success or fame, the gods have called him." For me, that about says it all. When you love what you're doing for its own sake, all the other details will take care of themselves. Sales is that kind of work for me. Here's hoping it is for you, too.

Good luck!

APPENDIX

On the following pages you will find model prospecting sheets, sales lead tracking sheets, and daily call report sheets. Use them!

PROSPECTING SHEET

CONTACT	CLASSIFICATION		
	A	B	C

PROSPECTING SHEET

CONTACT	CLASSIFICATION		
	A	B	C

PROSPECTING SHEET

CONTACT	CLASSIFICATION		
	A	B	C

_____

_____

_____

_____

_____

_____

_____

_____

_____

_____

_____

_____

_____

_____

_____

_____

_____

_____

_____

_____

_____

_____

_____

_____

PROSPECTING SHEET

CONTACT	CLASSIFICATION		
	A	B	C

PROSPECTING SHEET

CONTACT	CLASSIFICATION		
	A	B	C

PROSPECTING SHEET

CONTACT	CLASSIFICATION		
	A	B	C

SALES LEAD TRACKING SHEET

Name
_____

Telephone: /   -
_____

Address:
_____

Address:
_____

City: State: Zip:
_____

Contact person:
_____

DATE	CONTENT OF CALL	FOLLOW-UP	REMARKS

SALES LEAD TRACKING SHEET

Name
_____

Telephone: /   -
_____

Address:
_____

Address:
_____

City: State: Zip:
_____

Contact person:
_____

DATE	CONTENT OF CALL	FOLLOW-UP	REMARKS

SALES LEAD TRACKING SHEET

Name

Telephone: /   -

Address:

Address:

City: State: Zip:

Contact person:

DATE	CONTENT OF CALL	FOLLOW-UP	REMARKS

SALES LEAD TRACKING SHEET

Name

Telephone: /   -

Address:

Address:

City: State: Zip:

Contact person:

DATE	CONTENT OF CALL	FOLLOW-UP	REMARKS

SALES LEAD TRACKING SHEET

Name
_____

Telephone: /   -
_____

Address:
_____

Address:
_____

City: State: Zip:
_____

Contact person:
_____

DATE	CONTENT OF CALL	FOLLOW-UP	REMARKS

SALES LEAD TRACKING SHEET

Name
_____

Telephone: /   -
_____

Address:
_____

Address:
_____

City: State: Zip:
_____

Contact person:
_____

DATE	CONTENT OF CALL	FOLLOW-UP	REMARKS

SALES LEAD TRACKING SHEET

Name _____

Telephone: / - _____

Address: _____

Address: _____

City: _____ State: _____ Zip: _____

Contact person: _____

DATE	CONTENT OF CALL	FOLLOW-UP	REMARKS

SALES LEAD TRACKING SHEET

Name _____

Telephone: / - _____

Address: _____

Address: _____

City: _____ State: _____ Zip: _____

Contact person: _____

DATE	CONTENT OF CALL	FOLLOW-UP	REMARKS

SALES LEAD TRACKING SHEET

Name
_____

Telephone: /   -
_____

Address:
_____

Address:
_____

City: State: Zip:
_____

Contact person:
_____

DATE	CONTENT OF CALL	FOLLOW-UP	REMARKS

SALES LEAD TRACKING SHEET

Name
_____

Telephone: /   -
_____

Address:
_____

Address:
_____

City: State: Zip:
_____

Contact person:
_____

DATE	CONTENT OF CALL	FOLLOW-UP	REMARKS

SALES LEAD TRACKING SHEET

Name _____

Telephone: /   - _____

Address: _____

Address: _____

City: _____ State: _____ Zip: _____

Contact person: _____

DATE	CONTENT OF CALL	FOLLOW-UP	REMARKS

SALES LEAD TRACKING SHEET

Name _____

Telephone: /   - _____

Address: _____

Address: _____

City: _____ State: _____ Zip: _____

Contact person: _____

DATE	CONTENT OF CALL	FOLLOW-UP	REMARKS

DAILY CALL REPORT

Date: /   /

Page   of

Firm name/ location	Contact name/title Telephone number	Result	Follow-up?	Prospect category
_____				
_____				
_____				
_____				
_____				
_____				
_____				
_____				
_____				
_____				

DAILY CALL REPORT

Date: /   /

Page   of

Firm name/ location	Contact name/title Telephone number	Result	Follow-up?	Prospect category
_____				_____
_____				_____
_____				_____
_____				_____
_____				_____
_____				_____
_____				_____
_____				_____
_____				_____
_____				_____
_____				_____

DAILY CALL REPORT

Date: /   /

Page   of

Firm name/ location	Contact name/title Telephone number	Result	Follow-up?	Prospect category
————————				
————————————————————————				
————————				
————————————————————————				
————————				
————————————————————————				
————————				
————————————————————————				
————————				
————————————————————————				
————————				
————————————————————————				
————————				
————————————————————————				

Stephan Schiffman's Telemarketing

DAILY CALL REPORT

Date: / /

Page of

Firm name/ location	Contact name/title Telephone number	Result	Follow-up?	Prospect category

DAILY CALL REPORT

Date: /   /

Page   of

Firm name/ location	Contact name/title Telephone number	Result	Follow-up?	Prospect category
_____				
_____				
_____				
_____				
_____				
_____				
_____				

DAILY CALL REPORT

Date: /   /

Page   of

Firm name/ location	Contact name/title Telephone number	Result	Follow-up?	Prospect category
_____	_____			
_____	_____			
_____	_____			
_____	_____			
_____	_____			
_____	_____			
_____	_____			
_____	_____			

Share Your Comments!

I am always eager to hear your reactions to the programs I develop. If you have any comments or questions about the system I have outlined in this volume, please write me, Stephan Schiffman, care of Bob Adams, Inc., 260 Center Street, Holbrook, Massachusetts, 02343.

Index

FIND MORE ON THIS TOPIC BY VISITING
BusinessTown.com
The Web's big site for growing businesses!

- ☑ **Separate channels on all aspects of starting and running a business**
- ☑ **Lots of info on how to do business online**
- ☑ **1,000+ pages of savvy business advice**
- ☑ **Complete web guide to thousands of useful business sites**
- ☑ **Free e-mail newsletter**
- ☑ **Question and answer forums, and more!**

Accounting
Basic, Credit & Collections, Projections, Purchasing/Cost Control

Advertising
Magazine, Newspaper, Radio, Television, Yellow Pages

Business Opportunities
Ideas for New Businesses, Business for Sale, Franchises

Business Plans
Creating Plans & Business Strategies

Finance
Getting Money, Money Problem Solution

Letters & Forms
Looking Professional, Sample Letters & Forms

Getting Started
Incorporating, Choosing a Legal Structure

Hiring & Firing
Finding the Right People, Legal Issues

Home Business
Home Business Ideas, Getting Started

Internet
Getting Online, Put Your Catalog on the Web

Legal Issues
Contracts, Copyrights, Patents, Tradema

Managing a Small Business
Growth, Boosting Profits, Mistakes to Avoid, Competing with the Giants

Managing People
Communications, Compensation, Motivation, Reviews, Problem Employees

Marketing
Direct Mail, Marketing Plans, Strategies, Publicity, Trade Shows

Office Setup
Leasing, Equipment, Supplies

Presentations
Know Your Audience, Good Impression

Sales
Face to Face, Independent Reps, Telemarketing

Selling a Business
Finding Buyers, Setting a Price, Legal Issues

Taxes
Employee, Income, Sales, Property, Use

Time Management
Can You Really Manage Time?

Travel & Maps
Making Business Travel Fun